UNCLE GEORGE
AND ME

UNCLE GEORGE AND ME

Two Southern Families Confront a
Shared Legacy of Slavery

By Bill Sizemore

Brandylane
PUBLISHERS OF BOOKS / SINCE 1985

Cover design by Michael Hardison
Front cover photos: istockphoto.com #518523147 by Kubkoo and a Civil War-era Map of western Mecklenburg County, Va.
Back cover photo: Uncle George Sizemore with the author in 2017.

ISBN: 978-1-947860-10-0
LCCN: 2018942473

Printed in the United States

Published by
Brandylane Publishers, Inc.

"Your country? How came it yours? Before the Pilgrims landed we were here. Here we have brought our three gifts and mingled them with yours: a gift of story and song—soft, stirring melody in an ill-harmonized and unmelodious land; the gift of sweat and brawn to beat back the wildness, conquer the soil, and lay the foundations of this vast economic empire two hundred years earlier than your weak hands could have done it; the third, a gift of the Spirit. Around us the history of the land has centred for thrice a hundred years; out of the nation's heart we have called all that was best to throttle and subdue all that was worst; fire and blood, prayer and sacrifice, have billowed over this people, and they have found peace only in the altars of the God of Right. Nor has our gift of the Spirit been merely passive. Actively we have woven ourselves with the very warp and woof of this nation,—we fought their battles, shared their sorrow, mingled our blood with theirs, and generation after generation have pleaded with a head-strong, careless people to despise not Justice, Mercy, and Truth, lest the nation be smitten with a curse. Our song, our toil, our cheer, and warning have been given to this nation in blood-broth-erhood. Are not these gifts worth the giving? Is not this work and striving? Would America have been America without her Negro people?

"Even so is the hope that sang in the songs of our fathers well sung. If somewhere in this whirl and chaos of things there dwells Eternal Good, pitiful yet masterful, then anon in His good time America shall rend the Veil and the prisoned shall go free."

– W.E.B. DuBois, *The Souls of Black Folk*, 1903

CONTENTS

Introduction

Genealogy is a hot area of study these days. All over America, people are digging into their family histories. They want to know where they came from, who their ancestors were, and what legacy those ancestors left behind.

Only sometimes, they don't.

Henry Louis Gates Jr., the Harvard historian, found that out the hard way during the second season of *Finding Your Roots*, his popular genealogy show on public television. The show features celebrities discovering their ancestry with the help of Gates and his research team.

One of the episodes in 2014 featured movie star Ben Affleck. Months after it aired, when a hacked e-mail exchange between Gates and a Sony Pictures executive went public, the world learned that Affleck had successfully lobbied Gates to omit a key fact about his family history: his great-great-great-grandfather was a slave owner.

The repercussions were severe. An internal PBS investigation determined that Affleck had exerted improper influence over the editorial process. The show's third season was postponed for several months while an independent genealogist and a fact-checker were added to Gates' staff. Gates issued a contrite public apology.

Affleck was embarrassed by the revelation about his slave-owning ancestor, he wrote on Facebook: "The very thought left a bad taste in my mouth."

But once his effort to censor the information became public, he was embarrassed on a much grander scale. And along the way, a prominent academic and a respected television network had their reputations sullied.

What's the lesson here? The subject of American slavery— and its continuing legacy, the nation's crippling racial divide—is a minefield. The very thought of it is something many of us don't want to deal with.

This book flies in the face of white America's refusal to come to grips with its racial history. Its premise is that confronting and acknowledging America's original sin is a crucial step in healing the deep wound slavery left on our national psyche.

I feel Ben Affleck's pain. My great-great-great-grandfather, like his, was a slave owner. Like him, I am embarrassed by it. But unlike him, I feel compelled to share the story with whoever will listen.

My discovery of my family's slave-owning past is burned into my memory. I was in Utah on a reporting assignment for my newspaper, the *Virginian-Pilot,* in 2009. I had a couple of hours to kill before boarding my flight home and decided to visit the world headquarters of the Mormon church in Salt Lake City, which features the world's largest genealogical library.

I strolled in and was greeted by a friendly volunteer, who asked what I'd like to know about my family history. I said I wondered if any of my ancestors owned slaves. I've never bought into the old adage that ignorance is bliss. On the contrary, I believe knowledge is power. If my family participated in slavery, I wanted to know about it—for better or worse.

Within minutes, there was the answer on a computer screen in front of me: a slave schedule from the 1860 US Census showing my ancestor as the owner of sixteen people. I felt like I'd been punched in the gut.

From that moment forward, I couldn't get that discovery out of my mind. I was full of questions. Who were these people? What were their lives like? Who were their descendants? Where are those descendants now? What scars do they bear from their ancestors' enslavement? And perhaps the question that filled me with the most dread: am I related to any of them?

My curiosity led me on a years-long odyssey. The result is this book. It is the story of my ancestors, their slaves and those slaves' descendants. It is also, in microcosm, the story of Virginia, my native state; and of the South. Some of the touchstones of that story are well known; some are lesser known; and some lay buried for a century and a half, out of sight and out of mind.

Crucial to the story, of course, is the Civil War, that ghastly conflagration that tore the nation apart and put its founders' high-sounding ideals to an unimaginably bloody test. But just as important, I believe, is what came after that war: the dawn of freedom for the emancipated slaves, the brief taste of biracial democracy ushered in by the Reconstruction era, the viciously racist reaction from defeated Southern whites, the disfranchisement and humiliations of Jim Crow, the Great Migration of African-Americans out of the South in search of a better life, the halting gains of the civil rights era, and the persistent racial disparities that still plague the nation today.

The central characters in the Sizemore saga are one remarkable family of African-Americans who descended from two generations of my ancestor's slaves. Their family and mine, once so closely intertwined, had long been isolated from each other by the veil of segregation. For them and me, this odyssey has been a mutual journey of discovery. It has been a delight getting to know them over years of one-on-one visits and meet-ups at family reunions. Their stories form a complex tapestry with disparate threads of joy, struggle, hope, and despair. Some of them bear deep scars from past traumas. Some devised ingenious strategies for surviving the cruelties of Jim Crow. Some were on the front lines when the South's long-entrenched color barriers started to fall. One discovered a life-changing family secret that had been hidden for decades. Together they have wrestled with knotty issues of identity, religion, and sexuality.

Through it all, they have shown amazing resilience and resolve. They dealt with the indignities of second-class citizenship in different ways. Many joined the Great Migration; some stayed in the South. Their family ties became splintered in the process, but they have gone to great lengths to restore and nourish them, and from that they have drawn great strength. The older generations gladly made sacrifices to ease the way for their children and grandchildren. When they get together, the glow of family love is palpable.

They are an inspiration.

* * * * *

As I write these words, the vitriolic diatribes of recalcitrant racists ring in my head. For years I winced as I read their online comments reacting to my newspaper's coverage of racial issues. They didn't want to hear about how disadvantaged African-Americans were. A common refrain was "Why can't they just get over it?"

That attitude seems to persist like a pestilence rooted deep in the nation's soul, oblivious to a torrent of evidence that America is nowhere close to a postracial society. One need look no further than the near-daily accounts of white police officers gunning down young unarmed black men.

There is a vicious cycle at work. Consider what happened after a young white man killed nine worshipers during a prayer service at a historic black church in Charleston, South Carolina, in June 2015. The suspect in the massacre had posted a racist manifesto online replete with photos of himself posing with a handgun and a Confederate battle flag. His actions prompted discussions throughout the South about removing the Confederate flag from public spaces. Then, as surely as night follows day, came the howls of outrage from defenders of Southern "heritage" and a profusion of defiant new displays of the Stars and Bars flying from pickup trucks and front-yard flagpoles.

W.E.B. DuBois said it more than one hundred years ago: "The problem of the twentieth century is the problem of the color-line." Sadly, it is also the problem of the twenty-first century.

What the racists fail to grasp is that unlike whites, African-Americans still live with the legacy of slavery every day. They can't escape it. I once heard Christy Coleman, co-CEO of the American Civil War Museum in Richmond, put it this way: "You can't keep telling African-Americans, 'Get over it.' It's intrinsic to who we are."[1]

Now that I know the history of my family's involvement in slavery, I can't "just get over it" either. It's not that I feel personally guilty for my ancestors' sins. But I do feel a responsibility to help the nation overcome the lingering legacy of the cruel and inhumane system from which my family benefited. My hope is that this book will, in some small measure, help point the way to a more meaningful and productive national conversation about slavery and what it did to us as a people, black and white.

It is not the first book of its kind. There have been others, notably Edward Ball's *Slaves in the Family,* published in 1998. More recent examples are *Tomlinson Hill* by Chris Tomlinson, published in 2014; *Something Must Be Done About Prince Edward County,* by Kristen Green, in 2015; and *The Family Tree: A Lynching in Georgia,* by Karen Branan, in 2016. I am indebted to those authors for plowing the ground I trod. There is at least one key difference between their stories and mine, however. Until now, most of those accounts have dealt with large plantations that had hundreds if not thousands of slaves. Such massive operations were exceptional. Far more common were smaller, unremarkable farms like my ancestor's with fewer than twenty slaves. The stories of those slaveholders, most of which have not been told, illuminate the universality of the system and help explain why it was so difficult to eradicate. In thinking of them, I am reminded of Hannah Arendt's memorable phrase "the banality of evil."

The story of race is the story of America. I believe it is the responsibility of all Americans who care about the future of our nation to come to grips with it.

—1—

The Land of Eden

In a history of Mecklenburg County, Virginia, published in 1922, a local amateur historian opined, "No great historic event ever occurred in Mecklenburg."[2]

The Occaneechi Indians, however, might have begged to differ.

Mecklenburg County hugs the North Carolina border in the heart of Virginia's rural Southside, a region of gently rolling hills midway between the Atlantic coastal plain and the Blue Ridge Mountains. In the western end of the county, at the present-day town of Clarksville, the Dan and Staunton rivers merge to form the Roanoke River, which—with construction of a dam in the mid-twentieth century—became a sprawling lake known variously as John H. Kerr Reservoir and Buggs Island Lake.

At the confluence of the two rivers lay a string of islands, now submerged by the lake, blessed with rich alluvial soil ten feet deep, which had been deposited over the centuries by periodic floods.[3] For hundreds of years, the biggest of those islands—at four miles long—was home to the Occaneechis, a tribe whose power and wealth belied its small numbers.

Thanks to its strategic location astride a well-trod Indian trading path, the Occaneechis' fortified village served as a central trading mart for Indians for at least five hundred miles around.[4] They were only the latest in a string of indigenous peoples who had inhabited the Roanoke valley for thousands of years, but the Occaneechis were cursed with a fatal distinction: they were the first to encounter Europeans.

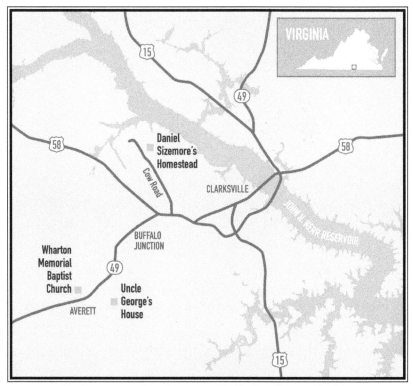

The Sizemore saga is set in western Mecklenburg County, Virginia, near the town of Clarksville.

English explorer Edward Bland wrote glowingly in 1650 about the Occaneechis' island home, which, he said, "is of a very rich and fertile soile."[5] Their fort was surrounded by lush peach orchards and immense fields of corn, beans, and squash. Virginia's colonial governor, William Berkeley, tried to foster peaceful coexistence with the colony's native tribes, but not all European settlers shared his go-along-to-get-along philosophy. One notable dissenter was Nathaniel Bacon, a hotheaded scion of a prominent English family who came to Virginia in 1674 to escape prosecution for fraud. He bought a plantation on the frontier near the falls of the James River and soon began attacking any Indians who got in his way.[6]

"In Bacon's mind, killing Indians was not just desirable and permissible but literally a patriotic duty," historian Ethan Schmidt has written.[7] After Susquehannock Indians attacked Bacon's farm and killed his overseer in 1676, Bacon recruited an illegal force of three hundred armed men to go after them in defiance of the governor's orders.

The Susquehannocks had established two encampments on the Roanoke River near the Occaneechis' island. Bacon's men followed them, arriving at the Occaneechi village in May 1676. The Occaneechis welcomed the Englishmen, brought them into the fort, and fed them.

At Bacon's urging, Occaneechi warriors attacked one of the Susquehannock camps, wiping out most of its 150 inhabitants. They brought the scalp of the Susquehannock chief back to Bacon along with seven prisoners, who were tortured and killed at Bacon's request.[8]

But Bacon wanted more. He demanded a share of the beaver pelts the Occaneechis had plundered from the Susquehannocks, along with provisions for his trip home. The Indians resisted Bacon's demands, and in the ensuing standoff a shot rang out behind Bacon, killing one of his men. Bacon retaliated with a brutal assault on his Occaneechi hosts. The Englishmen killed men, women, and children indiscriminately and set fire to the fort. Many Occaneechis burned to death or were blown up when the flames reached the powder stores. Those who escaped the burning buildings were cut down by gunfire. By some estimates, as many as three hundred Occaneechis died in the attack. Only a handful escaped the slaughter and abandoned the town.

What became known as Bacon's Rebellion has been described by historians as the first armed uprising in colonial America and a key turning point in the push for European dominance over the continent's native inhabitants.[9] The rebellion "helped establish the right of all Virginians to use violence against Native Americans whenever they deemed it necessary," Schmidt wrote.[10]

Among Bacon's early allies and drinking companions was William Byrd I, who had immigrated to Virginia from England four years before Bacon. By one account, it was Byrd—after a night of carousing—who persuaded Bacon to move against the Indians without the governor's authorization. But the politically savvy Byrd ultimately switched his allegiance to Berkeley, paving the way for a long and lucrative career as a planter, explorer, legislator, and trader with the Indians.

Byrd eventually gained title to nearly thirty thousand acres of land, which he passed on to his descendants. His son, William Byrd II, surveyed the line dividing Virginia and North Carolina, in exchange for which he acquired still more land in the region. He referred to his vast holdings as the Land of Eden.[11] In a 1733 account of his explorations, Byrd II wrote fondly of his ten-mile-long spread along the Roanoke River with its "three charming islands," including the Occaneechis' onetime home, where some of their peach trees still stood in the loamy soil more than half a century after the tribe's annihilation.[12]

Byrd II's son, William Byrd III, was a high-living gambler who systematically squandered the family fortune. In 1755, in dire financial straits, he conveyed his estate to seven trustees, who sold off land and slaves worth forty thousand pounds—a huge sum that still did not pay off all his debts. He committed suicide in 1777 at age forty-eight.[13]

In 1765, Byrd's trustees sold three thousand acres of his Roanoke River holdings—including Occaneechi Island—to Sir Peyton Skipwith, an American-born English baronet who established a sprawling tobacco plantation there. On a hill above the river's north shore with a commanding view of the verdant valley, Skipwith built Prestwould, a three-story mansion of hewn rose-colored native stone. The house survives today, remarkably intact, along with several outbuildings including a slave dwelling.[14]

The Prestwould mansion was built across the river from Daniel Sizemore's farm, near Clarksville, VA, by English baronet Sir Peyton Skipwith.

* * * * *

The few survivors of the Occaneechi massacre joined remnants of two related tribes, the Tutelo and Saponi, in a decades-long search for a new place to put down roots.

"Homeless wanderers on the face of the earth," John Tisdale, a longtime Mecklenburg County judge, called them in a 1953 history of the tribe. "What crime had these Children of Nature committed that would justify such horrible punishment? . . . Their only crime was that they stood across the path of the ambitions of stronger men."[15]

By 1700, Virginia's native population had plummeted to barely 1,400. They had lost much of their land to English squatters and had been devastated by disease, war, and slave traders.[16]

The surviving Occaneechis and their kinsmen migrated south to the Eno River in North Carolina. A decade later, they returned to Virginia and settled in Brunswick County under the protection of Governor Alexander Spotswood, who employed a teacher to educate and Christianize them. Within a few years, though, the

English halted their support of the settlement and the Indians abandoned it and scattered.

In the twentieth century, Virginia essentially defined its native inhabitants out of existence. The Racial Integrity Act of 1924 established two—and only two—rigid racial classifications. "Whites" were those without a trace of non-Caucasian blood. All others were "colored,"[17] including Indians, who thus were forced to endure the same indignities of segregation as African-Americans. (Later, the state amended the law in a concession to Virginians with ancestral ties to the celebrated Indian princess Pocahontas, who supposedly saved Captain John Smith's life and later married English settler John Rolfe. What became known as the "Pocahontas exception" to the Racial Integrity Act allowed those with no more than one-sixteenth Native American blood to be classified as white.)

In addition to defining "white" and "colored," the law criminalized marriage across racial lines—a prohibition that endured until it was overturned by the US Supreme Court in the 1967 case *Loving v. Virginia*.

Today a small community claiming historical descent from the Occaneechis lives in Alamance County, North Carolina, fifty miles from their old island home. Calling themselves the Occaneechi Band of the Saponi Nation, they are making a determined effort to keep their culture alive. They have hosted an annual powwow since 1995.

A former chief of the tribe, John "Blackfeather" Jeffries, told me it was "Eurocentric thinking" that conflated Indians and African-Americans. But there will come a time, he predicted, when all the old racial classifications will be moot.

"I guess if we live to the year 3000, we'll all be one race," he said. "The heart has no color."[18]

The great radical singer-songwriter Pete Seeger captured that thought in his slyly subversive song "All Mixed Up," written in the 1960s:

You know this language that we speak
Is part German part Latin and part Greek
With some Celtic and Arabic and Scandinavian all in the heap
Well amended by the people in the street
Choctaw gave us the word Okay
Vamoose is a word from Mexico way
And all of this is a hint, I suspect
Of what comes next

. . .

There were no redheaded Irishmen
Before the Vikings landed in Ireland
How many Romans had dark curly hair
Before they brought slaves from Africa?
No race on earth is completely pure
Nor is anyone's mind and that's for sure
The winds mix the dust of every land
And so will woman and man

. . .

I think that this whole world
Soon, mama, my whole wide world
Soon, mama, my whole world
Soon, gonna be get mixed up[19]

Today, of course, that mixing-up is happening before our very eyes. Multiracial families—the big bugaboo of generations of racists—are becoming commonplace.

It is the worst nightmare of Walter Ashby Plecker, Virginia's registrar of vital statistics from 1912 to 1946. The Racial Integrity Act's most zealous enforcer, he was a staunch promoter of eugenics, the now-discredited movement—emulated by Nazi Germany—that sought to provide a pseudoscientific basis for white supremacy. Plecker devoted his life to propagating the biological fiction of inherent racial differences—the philosophical pillar on which slavery was built.

Today, we know better. Anthropologists tell us race is a cultural invention that has no scientific meaning. Scientists theorize that skin color—which occurs on a continuum from darkest to lightest—evolved as an adaptive trait linked to geography and the strength of the sun's ultraviolet rays.

Geneticists unraveling the mysteries of human DNA can now say definitively that race as a biological category makes no sense. We all evolved from the same small group of tribes that migrated out of Africa and colonized the world over the past one hundred thousand years. Each person shares 99.99 percent of the genetic material of every other person. When the small remaining sliver of variable DNA is examined, people from the same race can be more different from each other than people from different races.[20]

Whiteness is nothing more than a state of mind, James Baldwin once wrote: "those who call themselves white . . . have brought humanity to the edge of oblivion: because they think they are white, they cannot allow themselves to be tormented by the suspicion that all men are brothers."[21]

For a few decades after their first contact with Europeans, some Virginia Indians—including some of Chief Jeffries' ancestors—were sold into slavery. But as the native population dwindled, Virginia planters looking for forced labor turned increasingly to Africans.

British pirates brought the first load of "20. and odd" Africans, in John Rolfe's description, plundered from a Portuguese slave ship off the coast of Mexico, to Point Comfort at the mouth of the James River in 1619. The captives were dispersed to several points across the Virginia colony including the capital, Jamestown, just three miles from my house outside Williamsburg.

At that time, in the provocative phrasing of author Theodore W. Allen, there were no "white" people in Virginia. In his two-volume 2012 work *The Invention of the White Race*, Allen writes that the colonists considered themselves simply English, not "white." In a search of the colonial records, Allen could find not a single instance of official use of the word "white" as a symbol of social status before its appearance in a 1691 law.[22]

For most of the 1600s, the bulk of the manual labor required for the colony's agricultural and commercial enterprises was supplied by lower-class immigrants brought from Europe, mainly England, as bond laborers. For decades they and their African counterparts occupied the same half-free status: not lifetime inherited slavery but fixed-term indentured servitude.

Eventually, the planter elite figured out that lifetime slavery made better business sense. By the 1700s, enslaved African labor had become a cornerstone of the Virginia economy.

One big risk of that business model, of course, was the potential for insurrection. The planters minimized that risk by creating a new system of social control in which the primary badge of status was race.

Coincidentally, Allen and several other scholars have made the case that a catalyzing event leading to the creation of that system was Bacon's Rebellion, which continued for several months after the massacre of the Occaneechis. In September 1676, Nathaniel Bacon proclaimed liberty to "all Servants and Negroes," urging European and African laborers to unite and overthrow the colonial governor and his inner circle of wealthy planters. Bacon's men drove Governor Berkeley out of Jamestown and set the town afire. Bacon died of typhus and dysentery in October, and his insurrection was finally quashed by Berkeley's forces in January 1677.[23] But the Virginia elite made up their minds to prevent a replay of it. As historian Edmund S. Morgan put it: "The answer to the problem . . . was racism, to separate dangerous free whites from dangerous slave blacks by a screen of racial contempt."[24]

A series of laws passed in the early decades of the eighteenth century systematically stripped African-Americans of the rights and privileges of citizenship. They were barred from voting or holding public office, bearing witness against a white person in court, serving in the militia, owning a gun, or "lifting his or her hand" against a European-American, effectively denying blacks the right of self-defense.

Poor whites were exempt from all those strictures, and their status was further enhanced by being given a key role in policing the system of racial control. In 1727, special militia detachments known as "the patrol" were instituted to enforce the Virginia slave code. Their ranks were filled mostly by non-landowning whites, many of them former indentured servants. Generations of slaves came to dread the "patrollers" who roamed the roads restricting slaves' travel, breaking up religious gatherings and chasing runaways.

As the institution of slavery grew and became more entrenched, the potential for upward mobility increased for less affluent whites, who could aspire to become slave owners themselves. Aristocrats like Sir Peyton Skipwith amassed hundreds of African slaves to tend their crops and perform domestic chores. Far more common, however, were yeoman farmers with twenty or fewer slaves.

The nasty business of human bondage crossed all social strata. And my family was in the thick of it.

—2—

Original Sin

I spent sixty years on this Earth without a clue that I was descended from slave owners.

For someone who spent his entire professional life as a journalist—much of that time as an investigative reporter—it's a little embarrassing to make that admission. But there it is.

Why did it take me so long to figure it out? I don't know. I suppose some of the reasons are mundane: I was busy making a living and raising a family. But more than that, I think I was infected by a sort of historical amnesia—self-induced, perhaps—that has long held sway in my native South.

"We live in the United States of Amnesia," Michael Eric Dyson has written.[25] Barbra Streisand provided the refrain: "What's too painful to remember/we simply choose to forget."

Never once during my growing-up years in the 1950s and 1960s did my parents mention any history of slaveholding in my family. While researching this book, I surveyed my cousins, and in every case the response was the same: the subject never came up in their families, either.

Did our parents not know, or did they know but choose not to talk about it? My cousins believe they didn't know. I retain some skepticism on that point. But if my cousins are right, it means that by the time our parents' generation came along, barely half a century after slavery was abolished, it had already been erased from the family's collective memory.

Uncovering the story of my family's slave-owning past has been a little like trying to piece together a jigsaw puzzle with a blindfold on. My ancestors were simple country folk. In contrast to their patrician neighbors, the Skipwiths, who left a voluminous paper trail, the Sizemores left no written records. So I had to rely on public documents.

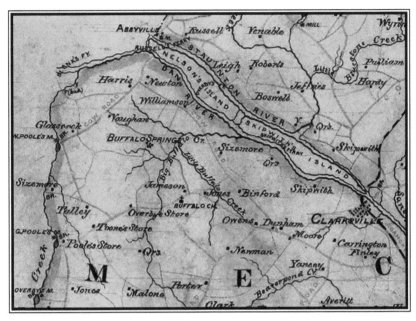

Two Sizemore farms are labeled on this Civil War-era map of western Mecklenburg County, VA. The slaveholder Daniel Sizemore's farm is in the center just below Skipwith's Island. His son Leroy Sizemore's farm is to the far left. The "Qr's" label designates slave quarters. / Library of Congress

My family's origins are a bit murky. There was a William Sisemore in the English colony at Jamestown as early as 1626, but no one has been able to trace my lineage back to him. My earliest known ancestor was a later William Sizemore, who turned up in Mecklenburg County in the latter half of the eighteenth century.

In 1772, seven years after Sir Peyton Skipwith acquired his massive Mecklenburg holdings from the dissolute William Byrd III, William Sizemore bought two hundred acres nearby on Great Buffalo Creek, a tributary on the south side of the Dan

River in sight of Occaneechi Island, which by then was known as Skipwith's Island.[26]

William Sizemore's granddaughter, Elizabeth, married my great-great-great-grandfather Daniel Sizemore, presumably a cousin of Elizabeth's, in 1809. Over the next four decades, Daniel Sizemore gradually acquired nearly five hundred acres on the south side of the Dan.[27]

He also acquired slaves. According to US Census records, he owned four slaves by 1840 and sixteen by 1860.[28] In this he was typical of the nearly four hundred thousand slaveholders across the South. Nearly nine out of ten had fewer than twenty slaves.

Slavery was well entrenched in Southside Virginia by the nineteenth century. Mecklenburg was one in a swath of counties south and east of Richmond that became known as the "black belt" because of its burgeoning slave population. By 1830, Mecklenburg's population was nearly two-thirds African-American.[29] The lists of slave owners include dozens of surnames that are still common in Mecklenburg. Among them: Blanks, Bugg, Boyd, Chandler, Crowder, Daniel, Elam, Gillespie, Griffin, Howerton, Ligon, Newton, Overbey, Puryear, Royster, Talley, Tarry, Toone, Watkins, Williamson, and Yancey.

By far the most lucrative money crop grown by Virginia's slave-owning planters was tobacco, which had been introduced from the West Indies by John Rolfe in 1612. Within a few decades, Virginia planters were producing millions of pounds of the golden leaf every year.[30] In those days, before the mechanization of agriculture, tobacco was an extremely labor-intensive crop, and therefore ideally suited for slave labor.

In a society dominated by the tobacco economy, my ancestors were no exception to the rule. They used slave labor to grow a highly addictive product that has killed millions of people all over the world. What a legacy!

Daniel Sizemore's house still stands on the land he farmed with sixteen slaves in 1860.

Daniel Sizemore and his wife are buried in a family cemetery near their farmhouse outside Clarksville, VA.

Daniel Sizemore's homestead—a modest clapboard house with a stone foundation, two rooms downstairs, and an upstairs loft—still stands today, surrounded by rolling pastureland along a centuries-old thoroughfare known as the Cow Road, three miles west of Clarksville. Daniel, his wife, and their son Harvel are buried in a family graveyard nearby.

According to the 1860 census, Daniel's slaves lived in three cabins on the farm. As far as I have been able to determine, there is no trace left of them, and no sign of where their inhabitants are buried.

* * * * *

A paroxysm of fear gripped Virginia's slave owners in August 1831 when Nat Turner, a slave preacher and prophet, led an army of seventy slave recruits on a deadly rampage through Southampton County, one hundred miles east of Daniel Sizemore's farm. Turner and his followers killed fifty-five white people before the insurrection was put down by state militiamen and federal troops, who killed some one hundred slaves, including some who took no part in the revolt. Turner, who believed God had chosen him to lead his fellow slaves to freedom, was put on trial and executed.[31]

That winter, amid the alarm ignited by Turner's rebellion, the Virginia legislature held a remarkably robust public debate on slavery. Over an extraordinary two weeks in January 1832, lawmakers wrestled with the moral, legal, and practical issues posed by the South's pervasive system of human bondage.

The debate broke down largely along geographic lines. Delegates from western Virginia, past the Blue Ridge Mountains, where slaveholding was rare, denounced the institution while those from the slave-dependent east defended it.

Mecklenburg's two delegates, William Goode and Alexander Knox, were among the leaders of the proslavery side. They portrayed slavery as a benign institution. Delegate James Gholson of Brunswick County, just east of Mecklenburg, declared Virginia's slaves "as happy a laboring class as exists upon the habitable globe."[32]

Impossible, responded Delegate William Preston of Montgomery, one of the western counties. "Happiness is incompatible with slavery," he said. "The love of liberty is the ruling passion of man; it has been implanted in his bosom by the voice of God."[33]

Mecklenburg's Knox, who ironically owned no slaves himself, nevertheless protested that he could not force his mind to the conclusion that slavery, as it existed in Virginia, was an evil. "On the contrary," he declared, "I consider it susceptible of demonstration that it is to this very cause that we may trace the high and elevated character which she has heretofore sustained; and, moreover, that its existence is indispensably requisite in order to preserve the forms of a republican government."[34] He looked to men's actions more than their words, Knox said, noting that Virginia's revered founding father Thomas Jefferson, despite his professed abhorrence of slavery, never liberated his own slaves, not even in death.

As for Jefferson himself, he had once written that maintaining slavery was like holding "a wolf by the ear, and we can neither hold him, nor safely let him go."[35]

Jefferson's lament found an echo in the Virginia debate of 1832. "For my own part, sir, I am not the advocate of slavery in the abstract," said Delegate John Brown of Petersburg, "and if the question were upon introducing it, I should be the very last to agree to it; but . . . it was cast upon us by the act of others. It was one of the attendant circumstances under which we were ushered into life. . . . It is our lot, our destiny—and whether, in truth, it be right or wrong—whether it be a blessing or a curse, the moment has never yet been, when it was possible for us to free ourselves from it."[36]

In the end, the legislature declared itself "profoundly sensible of the great evils arising from the condition of the colored population of this commonwealth," but concluded that abolishing slavery would be "inexpedient."

With that, Virginia doubled down on its embrace of slavery. Before adjourning, the legislature placed new restrictions on blacks' liberties, silencing black preachers, strictly regulating nighttime religious assemblies, constricting blacks' legal privileges, and prescribing fines and imprisonment for whites who tried to teach blacks to read.[37]

In Mecklenburg, white citizens met and drew up a manifesto proclaiming themselves *enemies even unto death* of all "who shall directly, or indirectly, undertake to rob us of our property, in our slaves, by word, act or deed."[38]

In the legislative elections that fall, several antislavery delegates were defeated. In Mecklenburg, proslavery stalwarts Goode and Knox were re-elected by large majorities. And at my alma mater, the College of William and Mary, a thirty-year-old history professor named Thomas Roderick Dew published a lengthy defense of slavery in 1832 that played a key role in hardening Southern opinion on the subject. "We have no hesitation in affirming," he wrote, "that slavery has been perhaps the principal means for impelling forward the civilization of mankind."[39]

Four years later, Dew ascended to the presidency of the college.

The debate was over. Virginia never again consulted its conscience about the morality of slavery. It would cling to the wolf's ear ever more tightly, not daring to let go.

* * * * *

What was life like for Daniel Sizemore's slaves? Put simply, I don't know. I have been unable to find historical accounts that shed any light on how they were treated. But there are dozens of firsthand narratives from other Virginia slaves, many of them collected by interviewers from the Federal Writers' Project in the 1930s, that tell of egregious cruelty and misery. Those accounts include frequent references to slave owners' most common method of discipline: flogging slaves' bare backs with a cowhide whip, sometimes for transgressions as small as stealing a candy cane or cutting a tobacco leaf before it was ripe.

The practice of flogging received a scientific veneer in 1851 when Dr. Samuel Cartwright, a Louisiana plantation physician, explained the tendency of slaves to flee captivity as a psychiatric condition he called "drapetomania." The term was derived from the Greek *drapetes*, or "runaway," and *mania*, or "madness." Cartwright suggested in a medical journal that slave owners could cure this "medical disorder" by whipping slaves and amputating their toes.[40] The whippings—administered by the slave owner himself, an overseer, or "patrollers" who roamed the countryside looking for runaways—were often lengthy and unmerciful, leaving the slave's back shredded and bloody. The standard treatment for a lacerated back was a rubdown with a concoction of salt, mustard, pepper, and vinegar that was thought to heal the skin without scarring, which helped disguise malcontents at slave auctions. Many slaves said it hurt worse than the whipping itself.[41] Minnie Folkes, who was enslaved in Chesterfield County near Richmond, told of watching her mother being whipped by an overseer. He tied her arms together over her head, suspended her from a beam in the barn, and flogged her naked back "'til the blood run down her back to her heels."[42]

Fannie Berry, who was enslaved in Appomattox County northwest of Mecklenburg, told of seeing a slave on a neighboring plantation tied to a tree and beaten to death by an overseer for killing a hog. Berry also told of her Aunt Nellie, who, after enduring a whipping by patrollers, told her niece, "Fannie, I done had my las' whippin'. I'm gwine to God." That night, she climbed to the top of a hill and hurled herself to her death on the rocks below.[43]

How widespread was flogging? It's hard to quantify, but it was certainly commonplace. Even the venerated soldier Robert E. Lee ordered three of his slaves stripped to the waist and given fifty lashes for attempting to flee to Maryland in 1859, according to a later account by one of the three.[44]

Another common theme in the slave narratives was the breakup of slave families by owners who sold spouses, siblings, and children to slave traders, who in turn sold them to cotton, rice, and sugar planters in the Deep South. Slave auctions were held in towns throughout slaveholding Virginia, none more than in Richmond, which became the largest slave-trading center in the upper South by the 1840s. The slave narratives contain wrenching accounts of young children being torn from their sobbing mothers' arms. Most never reconnected with their kin again.

Many slaves turned to religion as a refuge, yearning for release from their earthly woes in the afterlife. But slave owners did their best to extinguish religious gatherings of slaves, fearing they would be breeding grounds for insurrection. West Turner, who was enslaved in Nansemond County, now part of Suffolk in southeastern Virginia, recalled how patrollers routinely broke up slaves' religious meetings, telling them, "If I ketch you here servin' God, I'll beat you. You ain't got no time to serve God. We bought you to serve us."[45]

White preachers sometimes ministered to slave congregations, but more often than not exhorted them to accept their place and obey their masters. "It does not take a seminary education to know that white missionaries and preachers were distorting the gospel in order to defend the enslavement of blacks," the eminent African-American theologian James H. Cone has written. "Black slaves were condemned to live in a society where not only the government but 'God' condoned their slavery."[46]

The Baptist church, the dominant denomination in Southside Virginia and the one in which I was raised, had an antislavery stance before the American Revolution but had reached an accommodation with the institution by the nineteenth century. One Baptist pastor in Isle of Wight County, east of Mecklenburg, so riled his congregation with his antislavery views that he was attacked by a mob, his head dunked into mud until he almost drowned. He soon fled Virginia for Kentucky.[47]

The Southern Baptist Convention, now the largest Protestant denomination in the United States, was formed in 1845 in a split with Northern Baptists over whether slaveholders could be ordained as missionaries.

The Methodists and Presbyterians also split over slavery, but reunited in the twentieth century. The Baptists never did. It wasn't until 1995 that Southern Baptists adopted a resolution renouncing their racist roots and apologizing for their past defense of slavery, segregation, and white supremacy. In 2012, the denomination elected its first black president.

In addition to physical and social violence, the brutality and dehumanization faced by African American slaves extended to sexual violence. The slave narratives contain many accounts of female slaves being forced to have sex with their masters, often resulting in the birth of a child who then became the master's property. By law, slave children were classified as the property of their mothers' owners. Robert Ellett, who was a slave in King William County in eastern Virginia, remembered it this way: "In those days if you was a slave and had a good-looking daughter, she was taken from you. They would put her in the big house where the young masters could have the run of her."[48]

The sexual exploitation of female slaves was described in haunting detail by Harriet Jacobs, whose 1861 autobiography told the dramatic story of how she hid in an attic for seven years before making her escape to freedom. She was enslaved in Edenton, North Carolina, 150 miles southeast of Daniel Sizemore's farm. From the time she turned fifteen, Jacobs wrote, her master, a physician, "began to whisper foul words in my ear. . . . He peopled my young mind with unclean images, such as only a vile monster could think of. I turned from him with disgust and hatred. But he was my master. I was compelled to live under the same roof with him—where I saw a man forty years my senior daily violating the most sacred commandments of nature. He told me I was his property; that I must be subject to his will in all things. My soul revolted against the mean tyranny. But where could I turn for protection? No matter whether the slave girl be as black as ebony or as fair as her mistress. In either case, there is no shadow of law to protect her from insult, from violence, or even from death; all these are inflicted by fiends who bear the shape of men."[49]

I would of course like to think my ancestor treated his slaves humanely. But Jacobs' story gives me little reason to hope.

After recording a particularly gruesome litany of slave owners' cruelties—including the torture of a runaway slave who was locked inside a cotton gin and left to die—Jacobs wrote, "I could tell of more slaveholders as cruel as those I have described. They are not exceptions to the general rule. I do not say there are no humane slaveholders. Such characters do exist, notwithstanding the hardening influences around them. But they are 'like angels' visits—few and far between.'"[50]

Moreover, Jacobs wrote, slave owners were under no illusions about the morality of the institution that enriched them. She described one master on a neighboring plantation who appalled his friends with the shrieks and groans he uttered on his death-bed. His last words were "I am going to hell; bury my money with me."[51]

Frenchman Alexis de Tocqueville, who toured America in the 1830s and reported his observations in the widely read book *Democracy in America,* summed up Southern slaveholders this way: "From birth, the southern American is invested with a kind of domestic dictatorship . . . and the first habit he learns is that of effortless domination . . . [which turns] the southern American into a haughty, hasty, irascible, violent man."[52]

This detail from an 1860 census slave schedule describes Daniel Sizemore's sixteen slaves by age, sex, and race.

But even if my ancestor was the kindest master imaginable, it doesn't mean I get a pass for my family's role in slavery. He was still a willing participant in a brutal and inhumane system. As the theologian Cone put it many years ago: ". . . the 'good' masters were in fact the worst, if we consider the dehumanizing effect of mental servitude. At least those who were blatant in their physical abuse could not so easily dominate the minds of black people. . . . The masters' efforts to induce such mental servitude was perhaps the worst of their crimes, and the 'kind' ones did it best."[53]

* * * * *

Because of the paucity of the historical record, I have been able to learn only the most rudimentary facts about the Sizemore slaves.

The census records, which provided the first confirmation of my family's slave-owning past, only took me so far. Through 1860, slaves are listed by age, race, and gender—but not by name. On the 1860 slave schedule for Mecklenburg County, under the line where Daniel Sizemore's name is entered in a delicate cursive script, are sixteen blank lines where his slaves' names ought to be. To the right are letters and numbers describing each slave, ranging from a forty-year-old woman to a four-year-old girl. In a column with the heading "color," they are designated either "B" for black or "M" for mulatto. The latter term comes from the Spanish word for "mule"—the offspring of a horse and donkey— an insinuation that blacks and whites were close to being separate species.[54]

Those sterile census pages are a testament to the federal government's complicity in slave owners' determination to dehumanize their human property.

It wasn't until the 1870 census, after emancipation, that ex-slaves' names were recorded. I found more than a dozen African-American heads of households living in Mecklenburg County between 1870 and 1900 with the surname Sizemore. It's well known that freed slaves sometimes took the last name of their former owners, and since my ancestor was the only slave owner in Virginia named Sizemore, there's nowhere else that name would have come from.

So thanks to those later census records, I can recite the names of the enslaved Sizemores: Alex. Alice. Andrew. Ben. Berta. Booker. Daniel. Dennis. Henderson. Henry. Isham. Martha. Peter. Stephen. Wilkins.

Most of them married and had families. But most of them had disappeared from the Mecklenburg census records by 1900, so with just a few exceptions, that's all I know about them.

One such exception comes in the form of a surviving court document—a rare record of my slave-owning ancestor's spoken words. In 1854, a dispute over two slaves sold by the administrator of an estate came to the Mecklenburg court. One of the witnesses was my great-great-great-grandfather, Daniel Sizemore. He testified that he had purchased "a Negro boy named Wilkins" from one George Avory in January 1841 for $675 in cash. The boy had been sold the previous year at public auction in Clarksville in settlement of an estate.

"I was present at the sale and heard of no objection to the sale," my ancestor testified. "If I had heard of any objections to the sale I would not afterwards have purchased the boy."[55]

It was a profound moment for me when I first encountered that passage in the longhand script of a court stenographer from a century and a half ago: my ancestor describing matter-of-factly, in his own words, how he bought a fellow human being.

As for Wilkins Sizemore, he next turns up in the 1870 census as a freedman, head of a family of six. He was forty-four then, so he would have been about fifteen when my ancestor bought him.[56]

Another 1854 entry in the Mecklenburg court records contains testimony from my ancestor in a case that illustrates how the fiction of race had taken hold as a guiding principle in ordering Southern society. At issue was the will of one John Roberts, who had left most of his estate—including slaves—to two dark-skinned daughters, Maggie and Pamelia. Other relatives had sued the executor of the estate, arguing that the two young women were the product of their mother's adulterous affair with a black man and were not entitled to an inheritance.

When the question was put to Daniel Sizemore on the witness stand, he replied, "I know Maggie and Pamelia when I see them. I don't think they are white. I think they are mulatto. They have thick yellow skin like mulattoes and their hair is curly."[57]

Daniel's son-in-law A.C. Cox provided similar testimony. Unfortunately, despite my efforts to locate additional documentation, I was unable to determine how the case turned out.

I did, however, find another surviving record from the pre-Civil War era, a slave birth register. It records the birth of a slave boy, Peter, on May 12, 1853, and lists his owner as Daniel Sizemore. Neither of the child's parents is listed.[58]

That is the only slave birth recorded under Daniel Sizemore's name. But there could well have been others that went unrecorded. Documentation of Virginia's slave population was sometimes less than complete. Consider this notation by the Mecklenburg commissioner of revenue in an 1860 slave birth register: "Wm. Townes had six negro children born at his plantation. Names and sex not recollected and I am compelled to close. I have no time to ascertain the particulars."[59]

I found no further record of Peter, the slave boy born on Daniel Sizemore's farm. But that is not surprising in light of the astronomical mortality rate among slave children, which one historian has conservatively estimated at 40 to 45 percent.[60] Little Peter probably never made it to adulthood.

—3—

The Lost Cause

By 1860, nearly four million men, women, and children were enslaved across the South. Of all the Southern states, Virginia had the largest slave population, nearly five hundred thousand. More than twelve thousand of those lived and toiled in Mecklenburg County.[61]

The investment in all that human property was immense. Slaves constituted 75 percent or more of most slave owners' net worth.[62] And the beauty of it, from the slave owner's perspective, was that the investment was self-propagating. There were 204 slave births recorded in Mecklenburg in 1859, dwarfing the 49 white births that year.[63]

Slaves were so plentiful that their owners often hired them out to other planters or commercial enterprises. The 1860 census listed 165 slave "hirelings" working in the R.H. Moss & Bros. tobacco factory in Clarksville.[64]

The factory, which no doubt was built with slave labor, was a hulking three-and-a-half-story brick structure perched atop a hill a few blocks from the Roanoke River. In the twentieth century it became home to a weekly newspaper, the *Clarksville Times,* which was edited by my father, and later by me. The building was listed on the National Register of Historic Places in 1978 but, sadly, it was demolished in 1980.

The *Tobacco Plant,* a nineteenth-century newspaper published in Clarksville, was full of notices about slave auctions and rewards posted for the capture of runaways. An example of the latter, from September 8, 1858, read: "$25 REWARD: Ran away from the subscriber, about the first day of June last, my negro man NELSON, about 50 years of age, about 6 feet high, very dark mulatto complexion, of slow gait, generally looking downward, with very large feet, slow of speech but remarkably intelligent, rather bad countenance, and with hair slightly gray in front. It is suspected that he is about Townesville, N.C., where he once lived. The above reward of $25 is offered for his apprehension and delivery to the subscriber, at his residence near Scottsburg Depot, in Halifax County, or his confinement in jail and information thereof. GEO. W. VENABLE."[65]

The Moss Brothers tobacco factory in Clarksville employed slave "hirelings" from neighboring farms to process tobacco. In the twentieth century, the building housed a weekly newspaper, the Clarksville Times, *where the author served as the editor for several years in the 1970s. /* Clarksville Regional Museum

The October 14, 1859, issue of the *Tobacco Plant* carried a dramatic account of slave resistance headlined "Tragical Occurrence—A Negro Killed." The story concerned Jack, a slave on the Richard Boyd farm not far from Daniel Sizemore's place.

Jack came upon the overseer, Spencer Mullins, in the act of "chastising" Jack's sister Betsy in a barn—"chastising" being slave owners' polite term for whipping slaves.

"Jack entered with a bludgeon in his hand, and ordered Mr. Mullins to desist, telling him that he should not whip her," the newspaper reported. With the overseer distracted, Betsy slipped away.

When Boyd, the landowner, arrived, he ordered Jack to take off his shirt, whereupon Jack ran off into the woods. He returned after dinner and approached Mullins with a stick in his hand, saying "he had come back to kill or be killed." He charged at Mullins, who fatally stabbed him four times with his pocketknife.

The jury ruled the slaying self-defense. The reporter ended the story with this businesslike observation, chilling in its inhumanity: "The loss to the master cannot be less than $1,600, for the deceased was a young man, commanded the highest market price."[66]

The next week's issue of the *Tobacco Plant* carried the alarming report of John Brown's raid on the federal arsenal at Harper's Ferry in what was then northwestern Virginia. With his small band of fellow abolitionists, Brown hoped to instigate a slave rebellion that would spread across the South. The insurrection was quickly put down by a detachment of federal troops under Lieutenant Colonel Robert E. Lee, and Brown was executed.

Nevertheless, the raid struck fear into the hearts of slave owners. A month later, at a citizens' meeting in Boydton, the Mecklenburg County seat, a resolution was adopted condemning "the recent outrage at Harper's Ferry," calling it an "unparalleled assault upon our rights" and recommending the immediate formation of two or more volunteer militia companies in the county.[67]

The *Tobacco Plant*, like newspapers all over the South, saw abolitionism for what it was: a dagger pointed at the heart of the Southern economy and slave owners' fortunes. Editors spared no vitriol in their rhetorical assaults on the movement. For example, one editorial published in December 1859 reacted to news that a planter in Warren County, North Carolina, adjacent to Mecklenburg, had freed ten of his favorite slaves in his will and bequeathed them $10,000.

"We always regret to hear of any Southern slaveholder liberating his slaves either by deed or will," the *Tobacco Plant* opined. "Our reasons are two-fold: First, we are thoroughly convinced that what is intended as a benefit and a blessing must prove to be an unmitigated curse to the objects of the master's bounty. Secondly, every act of manumission is to a certain extent a concession to the wicked and fanatical principles of Northern abolitionists."[68]

A year later, the election of Republican candidate Abraham Lincoln to the presidency sent the editor of the *Tobacco Plant* into near apoplexy. Lincoln's abhorrence of slavery had not yet led him to embrace abolition, but his critics in the South clearly saw it coming. The election results constituted a "deplorable national calamity" for the "sovereign States of the Confederacy," the *Tobacco Plant* proclaimed: Lincoln's "avowed political principles are war to the death against their peculiar domestic institutions."[69] The Republican Party's "cherished aim" was the ultimate extinction of slavery, the newspaper warned, and no state had a bigger stake in the matter than Virginia: "The magnitude of her interest in the slave institution is immense. . . . It is absolutely impossible that Virginia can remain in the Union, if the Cotton States secede."[70]

In a December 1860 editorial, the *Tobacco Plant* asserted that abolitionism had to be resisted at any cost: "The slavery agitation has, like a wasting fever, fed upon the vitals of this country for now full forty years, until its exhausting effects can no longer be sustained. It must be checked, and that decisively."[71]

Events seemed to be propelling America inexorably toward what the *Tobacco Plant* and other newspapers across the South predicted would be "an open and bloody rupture," all over the question of preserving an economic system built on forced labor. The editorials in those papers make this crystal clear: the conflict was about slavery. No one tried to hide that fact—not even the Confederacy's top leaders. Alexander Stephens, the Confederate vice president, declared in March 1861, "The new constitution has put at rest, forever, all the agitating questions relating to our peculiar institution—African slavery as it exists amongst us—the proper status of the negro in our form of civilization. This was the immediate cause of the late rupture and present revolution. . . . Our new government['s] . . . foundations are laid, its cornerstone rests, upon the great truth that the negro is not equal to the white man; that slavery, subordination to the superior race, is his natural and normal condition."[72]

To insist, as some Southern apologists still do today, that the split was about something else is to ignore history. Yet that's what I and generations of other Southerners were taught. One of many examples of the revisionist history we were taught can be found in this passage from a history of Mecklenburg County published in 1977: "The War was not, after all, fought over the question of slavery but over the rights of individual states versus the power of the Union; slavery was only a secondary issue."[73]

It sounds so high-minded, fighting a war over a philosophical issue like states' rights rather than something so distasteful and mercenary as slavery. But this rewriting of history simply doesn't hold up under scrutiny. It's called denial.

* * * * *

By the spring of 1861, secession fever was taking hold in Mecklenburg. On April 5, the *Tobacco Plant* reported that funds had been raised to hoist a secession flag in Clarksville.[74]

Confederate guns fired the opening volleys of the Civil War at Fort Sumter, South Carolina, on April 12. Finally, at a convention in Richmond on April 17, Virginia delegates voted to secede, a decision ratified by voters a month later.

On May 10, the *Tobacco Plant* reported that two infantry companies had formed in Clarksville and left by train for Richmond. "They go to the post of danger with stout hearts and determined spirits," the newspaper reported, "resolved to drive back the dastard invader from the consecrated soil of Virginia, or to die in the attempt."[75] One of those units, Company E of the Fourteenth Virginia Infantry, known as the Clarksville Blues, included Private Marvel Sizemore, a twenty-three-year-old grandson of my slave-owning ancestor Daniel Sizemore, then in his seventies.

Marvel was one of five sons of Daniel's son Leroy, an overseer on the W.P. Pool farm. Four of those sons ultimately went off to war. My great-grandfather Thomas Ledford Sizemore was the second to sign up, a mere month after Marvel left. Thomas was twenty-one.[76]

Thomas Ledford Sizemore (1840–1898), the author's great-grandfather, was injured in Pickett's Charge at the Battle of Gettysburg.

The two brothers joined the army voluntarily, but military service soon became mandatory. In 1862 the Confederacy enacted the first conscription laws in American history. There were a couple of loopholes, but none of the Sizemore boys could or would take advantage of them. Draftees could avoid service by paying a substitute to go in their stead, and one able-bodied white male was exempted from service for every twenty slaves owned by a household.[77]

Eli, the third Sizemore brother to enter the army,

in March 1862, never made it home to Mecklenburg. Within five months he died in Richmond's Chimborazo Hospital of disease, which killed more Civil War soldiers than combat. He was just nineteen.[78]

The Fourteenth Virginia Infantry was thrust into some of the bloodiest combat of the war, suffering significant casualties as it helped defend Richmond and ventured into Maryland in 1862. Marvel Sizemore saw action in a series of battles that year: Seven Pines, Malvern Hill, Manassas, Harper's Ferry, Antietam, Fredericksburg.[79] He was home on furlough when the Fourteenth joined the biggest battle ever fought in North America—at Gettysburg, Pennsylvania, in the summer of 1863. But his brother Thomas, my great-grandfather, was there.

Thomas—a wiry five feet six inches tall, fair-skinned, with red hair and hazel eyes—was wounded in the shoulder and captured by Union forces during Major General George Pickett's ill-fated charge up Cemetery Hill when the Confederate troops were mowed down by devastating cannon and rifle fire. Thomas returned to his unit in a prisoner exchange three months later.[80]

The carnage at Gettysburg—more than fifty thousand men killed or wounded on the two sides—is generally regarded by historians as the beginning of the end of the Confederacy. After the remnants of Pickett's troops fell back from their failed charge, General Robert E. Lee told Pickett to form up his division to repulse a possible Union counterattack. Pickett responded, "General Lee, I have no division."[81]

On the Fourth of July, Lee's forces began their desultory retreat to Virginia. The wagon train of wounded soldiers stretched more than fourteen miles.

A firsthand account of that trek by Confederate General J.D. Imboden was widely published after the war in Southern newspapers, including the *Mecklenburg Herald.* The train slogged through torrential rains, drenching the injured soldiers lying on the hard, naked boards of the wagons. They were "wounded and mutilated in every conceivable way," Imboden wrote—skulls cracked, legs shattered, arms torn to shreds. "The jolting was enough to have killed sound strong men," he wrote. From nearly every wagon rose shrieks: "O God! Why can't I die?" "My God! Will no one have mercy and kill me and end my misery?" Some prayed; some swore; from some wagons only low deep moans and sobs were heard. Many did, in fact, die before they reached home.[82]

The fourth Sizemore brother, Harper, enlisted in the Fourteenth Infantry in April 1864 at age nineteen and was immediately thrown into a series of battles around Richmond and Petersburg including the Battle of Drewry's Bluff, where his brother Marvel was wounded.[83]

The closest the war came to Mecklenburg County was at the Battle of Staunton River Bridge, a covered railroad bridge on the Halifax-Charlotte county line, in June 1864. There, a battalion of Virginia reserve troops successfully fended off Union forces trying to slice through a key supply line serving Lee's troops around Petersburg.

The reserves consisted of so-called "young boys and old men," ranging in age from seventeen to fifty. One of the "old men" was the Sizemore brothers' uncle Harvel, who joined up in July 1864 at age forty-two.[84]

* * * * *

The Sizemore slaves didn't escape service in the Confederate cause, either. Beginning in mid-1862, under orders from the Virginia legislature, Mecklenburg slave owners furnished hundreds of male slaves between the ages of eighteen and forty-five as laborers to work on the fortifications around Richmond, the Confederate capital. Surviving records indicate that as many as a half dozen of Daniel Sizemore's slaves were among them.[85] Their names are not recorded, but from other records we can surmise who some of them would have been. Wilkins, who had been bought as a teenager, would have been about thirty-six in 1862.

Three more male slaves were in the same age bracket: Daniel, who shared his owner's first name, was about twenty-eight; Henderson was twenty-nine; and Henry was eighteen. In all likelihood, they all were put to work fortifying the Confederate lines.

Slave owners were paid sixteen dollars per month per slave for the grueling work performed by their human property. Long lines of slaves labored on the trenches, swinging pickaxes and heaving dirt. Many became ill or exhausted. They were often brutally treated by their military supervisors. Some died.[86]

Any owner who refused to provide the requisitioned slaves was subject to a fine of ten dollars a day. Some were reluctant to comply, trying the patience of state and Confederate authorities. Their annoyance was apparent in Governor William Smith's order calling up one gang of slave laborers: "I earnestly hope prompt and immediate response to this call will be made, involving as it does the safety of the capital of our state, and, it may be, of the institution of slavery itself."[87]

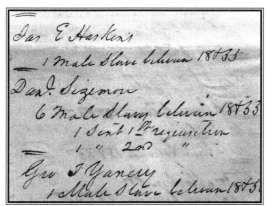

This Civil War-era document shows that some of Daniel Sizemore's slaves were requisitioned to work on Confederate fortifications around Richmond. / Library of Virginia

Letters poured in to the governor from slave owners asking to be compensated for impressed slaves lost to disease, accident, exposure, and neglect. "Have you ever noticed the strange conduct of our people during the war?" a Confederate congressman from Georgia asked. "They give up their sons, husbands, brothers and friends, and often without murmuring, to the army; but let one of their negroes be taken, and what a howl you will hear."[88]

The impressment of slaves as laborers in the Confederate war effort continued well after Lincoln's issuance of the Emancipation Proclamation on January 1, 1863, freeing slaves in the rebellious states. The proclamation ignited hope in the hearts of slaves, but the freedom it promised depended on a Union victory. In April 1863, ninety-eight Southern clergymen met in Richmond and issued a rebuttal to Lincoln's proclamation, assailing abolitionism as interference with God's plan for the improvement and salvation of the African race by its enslavement to Christians.[89]

Meanwhile, Southern authorities did everything in their power to tamp down slaves' hopes of liberty. In mid-1861, a slave named Sam on the Mecklenburg farm of John Winckler was put on trial for plotting insurrection. If the testimony of one witness is any guide, Sam's transgressions consisted of little more than loose talk. That witness, Robert Adams, said he heard Sam say, "I suppose we will all be free pretty soon. . . . From what I can find out, old Lincoln is coming down the Mississippi River and will free everything as he goes." The witness added, "He also said that if he could see every Southern man's head cut off, he would not put his hand near to save their lives."[90]

The evidence was good enough for the jury. Sam was found guilty and sentenced to be transported and sold beyond the borders of the United States.[91]

An even worse fate befell a slave named Uncle Toliver in Nansemond County, east of Mecklenburg. When his owner's two sons overheard him praying for the Yankee troops, they ordered him to kneel in the barnyard and pray for the Confederates instead. When he refused, the brothers took turns whipping him until he collapsed and died.[92]

Blacks were not allowed into combat roles in the Confederate forces until the closing weeks of the war, and none fought in Virginia. "Surely, they are good enough for Yankee bullets," one Virginia newspaper opined. But some Southern whites were apprehensive. "The day you make soldiers of them is the beginning of the end of the revolution," General Howell Cobb warned. "If slaves will make good soldiers our whole theory of slavery is wrong."[93] The Union, meanwhile, had been recruiting black troops since late 1862, and by the end of the war African-Americans accounted for 10 percent of the Union forces.

A division of the US Colored Troops, as they were known, marched into an appalling slaughter at the Battle of the Crater near Petersburg in August 1864, part of a nine-month-long stretch of trench warfare around the strategic city that became known as the Siege of Petersburg. Union forces tunneled under Confederate lines and planted explosive charges, which were set off in a massive blast that created a crater 170 feet long and 30 feet deep, killing several hundred Confederate troops instantly. But in a failure of leadership, Union troops—including the black division—were sent down into the crater, where they came under withering fire from Confederate troops around the rim as they tried to escape.

William Mahone / Library of Congress

The Confederate forces were under the command of General William Mahone, a diminutive railroad magnate and politician from southeastern Virginia who had moved his wife and children to Clarksville for their safety during the war. Horrified at the massacre of the black troops, Mahone and his subordinate officers tried to stop the slaughter, to no avail. The sight of the black troops "had the same effect upon our men that a red flag had upon a mad bull," one South

Carolina soldier wrote later. A North Carolina soldier described the grisly scene this way: "The soldiers were excited; they were reckless; they burst the negroes' skulls with the butts of their guns like eggshells."[94] Many of the black troops were killed after they had thrown down their arms, trying to surrender.[95] When the fighting was over, their bodies were reported to be lying eight to ten deep.

During the Civil War, this house on Sixth Street in Clarksville was home to the family of William Mahone, a Confederate general who later became a US senator and leader of the biracial Readjuster Party.

At a mass meeting called by black leaders in Boston after the carnage in the crater, a speaker cited reports of black soldiers "mown down like grass at Petersburg."[96] Ultimately, they suffered the highest casualty rate of any division in the battle.

For one pro-Confederate newspaper, that wasn't enough black blood shed. In an editorial after the battle, the *Richmond Examiner* had this advice for Mahone: "Shut your eyes, General, strengthen your stomach with a little brandy and water, and let the work, which God has entrusted to you and your brave men, go forward to its full completion; that is, until every negro has been slaughtered."[97]

The Siege of Petersburg came to a decisive end on April 1, 1865, when Pickett's Confederate forces were routed by Union troops at Five Forks, a key junction outside the city. Pickett had been attending a shad bake when the fighting began and was unaware a battle was underway until it was too late.

All three surviving Sizemore brothers were on the battlefield at Five Forks. Two of them, Thomas and Harper, were captured and imprisoned at Point Lookout, Maryland, until June, two months after the war ended.[98]

On April 2, the day after the Union victory at Five Forks, Lee informed Confederate President Jefferson Davis that Richmond and Petersburg would have to be evacuated. Just before Union forces swept in, Davis and his cabinet fled southwest to Danville, which for a few days became the last capital of the Confederacy.

Upon the fall of Richmond, throngs of cheering blacks lined the streets as Union soldiers marched in. From behind the barred windows of Lumpkin's Jail, operated by notorious slave trader Robert Lumpkin, imprisoned slaves began to chant:

Slavery chain done broke at last!
Broke at last! Broke at last!
Slavery chain done broke at last!
Gonna praise God till I die!

As the crowd outside took up the chant, soldiers opened the slave cells and the prisoners came pouring out, praising God and President Lincoln for their deliverance.[99]

On April 4, Lincoln and his son Tad visited the still smoldering ruins of Richmond. Ecstatic blacks swarmed around their carriage, waving handkerchiefs, hats, and bonnets and shouting praises to the man they called "Father Abraham." In a speech from the steps of the abandoned rebel Capitol, he told them, "God has made you free."[100]

Five days later, on April 9, Lee surrendered to General Ulysses Grant at Appomattox Courthouse, finally ending four years of horrific national fratricide. Among the Confederate soldiers laying down their arms at Appomattox was Private Marvel Sizemore, one of just fifty-seven men left in a regiment that once boasted seven hundred.[101]

The human cost of the war exceeded all expectations. The estimated 750,000 deaths eclipsed those of every other

American war before or since.[102] On the Mecklenburg County Veterans Memorial in Clarksville, which lists local soldiers killed in all those wars, the Civil War section is by far the largest, containing more than four times as many names as

Eli Sizemore's name appears on the Mecklenburg County Veterans Memorial in Clarksville. He died of disease at age 19, five months after enlisting in the Confederate army.

World War II, the next largest. Among the hundreds of names engraved there is that of Private Eli Sizemore.

The night before the surrender, Lee had discussed the South's plight with Mahone and his other generals. He is reported to have said, "Well, it is ended, and forever. Slavery disappears never to be known again. The wise thing is to accommodate ourselves to the new order of things, and go home and go to work." Lee's solemn words were said to have a profound impression on Mahone as he departed the battlefield to rejoin his family in Clarksville.[103]

For the South's four million former slaves, the dawn of freedom after more than two centuries of bondage was intoxicating. The great African-American scholar W.E.B. DuBois described the moment in a lyrical passage seventy years later:

"There was joy in the South. It rose like perfume—like a prayer. Men stood quivering. Slim dark girls, wild and beautiful with wrinkled hair, wept silently; young women, black, tawny, white and golden, lifted shivering hands, and old and broken mothers, black and gray, raised great voices and shouted to God across the fields, and up to the rocks and the mountains."[104]

But many Southern whites were not ready to accept Lee's advice to acquiesce in the new order of things. On April 15, as part of a conspiracy to revive the Confederate cause, the actor John Wilkes Booth assassinated Lincoln as he sat with his wife watching a play at Ford's Theatre in Washington.

It is impossible to say how things might have been different for the freed slaves if the Great Emancipator had lived. But this much is certain: The road to African-Americans' full enjoyment of the bounties of the American republic would be long and painful. A century and a half later, we are still not at its end.

—4—

Uncle George

Since the 1950s, my extended Sizemore family has held a reunion every August in the rural community near Clarksville where my father and his five siblings grew up. The event has had remarkable staying power. Dozens of my relatives across multiple generations show up every year, some traveling from as far away as the West Coast.

Sitting at my computer a few days before our 2010 gathering, I idly typed in a Google search for "Sizemore family reunion" and made a startling discovery. There was a rather elaborate website dedicated to an annual gathering of Sizemores—not my kin, but an African-American family.

In an amazing coincidence, their reunion is held on the same weekend each year as ours. Theirs migrates from year to year all over the Eastern Seaboard, but every few years it returns to the place of their roots: Mecklenburg County, Virginia.

When I was growing up there, every aspect of life was strictly segregated—schools, churches, clubs, public accommodations. I had little contact with African-Americans, and I had only the vaguest awareness that there were any who shared my surname.

My discovery of the simultaneous reunions came shortly after I had begun exploring my family's slave-owning past. Intrigued, I began seeking out African-American Sizemores, asking who could tell me about their family history. I was quickly steered to George Sizemore.

Uncle George, as everyone in his family calls him, lives in the same weathered farmhouse where he has lived since he was one month old in 1919, about five miles from where my ancestor Daniel Sizemore lived. He has been alone since Laura Mae, his wife of fifty-eight years, died in 2007.

Uncle George Sizemore has lived in this house outside Clarksville since he was one month old in 1919.

Soon after the two family reunions, I called Uncle George and asked if I could pay him a visit. He readily agreed. A few days later I parked behind his farmhouse and made my way to the back door across a concrete patio, eyed by several curious cats.

Uncle George answered my knock by throwing open the porch's screen door. He was a very vigorous ninety-one-year-old at the time—a towering figure at six feet four and 240 pounds, with a toothy smile and immense hands. When we shook hands, mine disappeared inside his.

He led me through the kitchen into a small den where he had been watching a ball game on a big-screen TV. I took a seat on the sofa.

I wasn't sure how to bring up the subject of slavery, but as it turned out, I needn't have worried. Uncle George was happy to discuss his family history. "All my family talk a lot," he told me with a sly grin. "I'm the quiet one." He then proceeded to talk nearly nonstop, prompted only by an occasional open-ended question from me. One of the first things he told me was "My daddy was born a slave."[105]

I had to let that sink in for a moment. How was it possible that in 2010, someone could be just one generation removed from slavery?

But once he explained it, I found the math worked out. Uncle George's father, Ben Sizemore, was born in 1858. He fathered six children with his first wife and, after she died, five more with his second wife. Uncle George was the next to last of those, born when his father was sixty-one.

The 1870 census shows white Daniel Sizemore and his adult children living next door to black Daniel Sizemore and his sons Ben and Stephen.

Uncle George told me that Ben and his brother Stephen were the sons of a slave named Daniel—the same name as that of my slave-owning ancestor. He used to have a portrait of his grandfather, he said. The picture unfortunately had been lost, but he still remembered it vividly. "He wasn't black and he wasn't white," Uncle George said. "He was fair-skinned, with slightly curly hair"—a marked contrast to Uncle George's deep brown complexion.

After that first of many visits with Uncle George, I went scurrying back to the census records. In the 1870 census, I found documentation of Uncle George's ancestors, along with an unmistakable link to my own. There, listed in Clarksville Township, are Daniel Sizemore, a thirty-six-year-old black farmworker, and his young sons Ben and Stephen. The listing appears immediately after that of my ancestor Daniel Sizemore, an eighty-one-year-old white farmer, and his four unmarried adult children. That means black Daniel and his sons lived next door to white Daniel, most likely in the same cabin they inhabited as slaves.[106]

A few lines down on the same census page are listings for another of white Daniel's children and three of his grandchildren, including my great-grandfather Thomas and his brother Marvel.

How did the black and white Daniel Sizemores come to have the same name? We can only guess. One question that naturally arises is whether there was any blood connection between the two. The answer, according to two pairs of DNA tests, is no.

Uncle George and I took a test focusing on the Y chromosome, which occurs only in males and is passed from father to son. The result: he and I have no shared male ancestor. Next, Uncle George's niece Eugene Watkins and I took an autosomal DNA test, which reveals blood relationships stretching out to distant cousins. No kinship was found there, either.

The autosomal test also reveals ethnic makeup. Mine was found to be 100 percent European. Eugene's is 85 percent African, 12 percent European, and 3 percent Native American. Traces of European ancestry are common among African-Americans, reflecting the widespread reality of slave owners mating with their female slaves.

Uncle George is no exception. He has white blood on his mother's side, he told me in one of our early conversations. When he was a boy, he noticed a curious bond between his mother, Ella Jamieson Sizemore, and two white brothers who ran a funeral business. There were no black undertakers in Mecklenburg County in those days.

Whenever there was a funeral in the neighborhood, the two white undertakers "would always hug my mama," Uncle George told me.

"I'd say, 'Mama, why are those white people always hugging you?' Finally, when I was a teenager, she told me: 'We're cousins.'"[107] Ella's mother, Uncle George's grandmother, born in 1857, had a white father.

Uncle George and his kin were mildly surprised—as was I—that the DNA tests turned up no biological connection between our families. I reported the results of our DNA testing to the African-American Sizemores at their 2011 family reunion. After a hearty dinner of fried catfish in a picnic shelter at a state park near Clarksville, I told the family there appeared to be no blood ties between us. At that, there was an audible sigh from the crowd. Was it relief? Disbelief? Disappointment? Perhaps it was a combination of all three.

The DNA tests, of course, tell us only about the two Daniel Sizemores and their progeny. There were more than a dozen other Sizemore slaves, and I have been unable to locate any of their descendants for testing. But one thing is crystal clear from the census records: for decades after emancipation, the lives of the black and white Sizemores were tightly intertwined. Up through 1900, they lived in close proximity. In all likelihood, the black Sizemores were sharecroppers working the same farmland on which they had toiled as slaves.

* * * * *

Every time I visit Uncle George, I learn something new.

He has remained vigorous well into his upper nineties. He still plants a garden every spring, growing tomatoes, cucumbers, peppers, and green beans, giving much of the produce away to friends and neighbors. He loves to sit under a big shade tree in his backyard in the early morning, listening to the birds and watching the sun come up. He finally gave up driving and now uses a walker to get around the house, but he drew the line when his doctor tried to put him on a diet. "I said, 'Are you kidding? I'm almost one hundred years old and you want to take my appetite away? I'll eat what I like.' I like to have some fried chicken sometimes. Friends bring me rabbit, squirrel, and deer they've killed and I cook it up. And I always have some pie and cake in the house."

Ben Sizemore, Uncle George Sizemore's father, was born a slave in 1858.

One thing he did give up—many years ago—was bootleg whiskey. He once imparted to me a lesson from his drinking years: how to tell whether a batch of moonshine is good or not. "When you shake it up, if the bubbles come up slow, it's good. If they come up fast, it's rotgut."

Uncle George told me his father, Ben, never talked much about the childhood he spent in slavery. But one incident was seared into Ben's memory. When he was a young boy, his father took him to see a hanging. Horrified by the grisly sight, the boy turned away and clung to his father's leg, hiding his eyes.

That was almost certainly the hanging of Fred, a slave on Tucker Carrington's farm, which wasn't far from Daniel Sizemore's. Fred had been put on trial in July 1864 along with another slave, Jesse, for plotting insurrection.[108]

A month earlier, after being rebuffed at the Battle of Staunton River Bridge, a Union cavalry force under General James Wilson had moved eastward through northern Mecklenburg County. They stopped at Carrington's plantation, where the slave Fred joined them. The Yankee cavalrymen next stopped at Dr. John Boswell's plantation, where, according to testimony, Fred told them where to find Boswell's hidden mules.

Jesse, a slave owned by Rebecca Wagstaff, was visiting his wife at the Boswell plantation when the federal troops arrived and enlisted his help. According to testimony, Jesse was reluctant at first, but he became more cooperative when the Union force reached the next house, owned by Robert Burton. The cavalrymen broke into the house and took sugar and clothing, sharing the spoils with the two slaves. Fred donned Burton's pantaloons and Jesse put on his greatcoat.

At the trial, Fred was quickly convicted on a felony count of conspiring "to rebel and to make insurrection" and was ordered to be "hanged by the neck until he be dead" on August 26, 1864.[109] Uncle George's father would have been about six years old then.

Fred was one of 628 slaves executed by Virginia authorities between 1785 and 1865. Untold thousands more were ordered whipped or given other corporal punishments.[110]

One of those was Jesse, the slave tried with Fred. He was acquitted of the felony charge but convicted of a misdemeanor and ordered to be given "thirty nine lashes upon his bare back to be well laid on."[111]

* * * * *

Aside from DNA evidence (or the lack of it), trying to trace African-American family roots is a frustrating exercise. In most cases, the paper trail only goes back to 1870, when the freedmen's names first appeared in census records. For many present-day African-Americans, the most that can be said about their earlier ancestors is that they came from somewhere on the vast continent of Africa.

An estimated ten million Africans were brought to the Americas over 350 years. As many as one in eight perished on the Middle Passage across the Atlantic Ocean, chained together in the fetid holds of slave ships under horrific conditions.

Those who survived the voyage were systematically stripped of everything they had: their freedom, of course; but also their names, their families, their language, and their culture. In their terrifying new world as human chattel, their life stories began anew on a blank slate.

A side note: I've learned that roadblocks in genealogical research are not confined to African-Americans. The DNA tests in which I participated exposed similar uncertainties about my own family origins.

Three of my cousins took the same Y-chromosome test that I took. As expected, we all match up in the results. But in an unexpected twist, we don't match any of the other male descendants of European-American Sizemores who were living in Mecklenburg and Halifax counties at the turn of the nineteenth century. Instead, we match a large number of people with the surname Vaughan or Vaughn. The inescapable conclusion is that our paternal ancestor a generation or two before Daniel Sizemore was not a Sizemore, but a Vaughan.

Census records and maps from the period show that there were in fact several Vaughan households living in close proximity to the Sizemores. Was there an adoption? An extramarital relationship? I don't know. So far, it is a mystery without a solution.

The DNA results even cast doubt on my ancestral nationality. Since Sizemore is unquestionably an English surname, my relatives and I always assumed we came from English stock. But the Vaughan name originated in Wales. So it appears we are at least part Welsh.

* * * * *

That mystery aside, I was thrilled to find additional documentation of the African-American Sizemores' ancestors in records of the Freedmen's Bureau. That agency, established by Congress in March 1865 as the Civil War drew to a close, was charged with overseeing and facilitating ex-slaves' transition to freedom. It was short-lived, but for a brief moment in history it brought an unprecedented experiment in interracial democracy to every corner of the South, including Mecklenburg County. Among other things, the bureau provided freedmen with food and clothing, medical attention, and help securing education and employment—all against a backdrop of ill will and resistance from their former masters.

"The citizens seem to wish for the extermination of the Negro," John Guilfoyle, the assistant superintendent in the bureau's Clarksville office, wrote to his superiors on December 14, 1865. ". . . There is a very bad spirit existing between the Freedmen and their former owners. . . . The freedmen appear to be trying to do the best they can such as getting new situations, renting lands, etc., which the citizens are very much opposed to in many cases."[112]

One function of the Freedmen's Bureau was the formalizing of slave marriages, which had no legal sanction before emancipation. Those unions, many of them longstanding, were recorded by bureau agents in cohabitation registers.

Uncle George had told me that his grandmother, Daniel Sizemore's common-law wife, was named Page. I have found her listed variously as Page and Patience in census, birth, and marriage records. The earliest such record appears in a Freedmen's Bureau cohabitation register, probably compiled in 1865 or 1866. The handwritten list includes the union of Daniel Sizemore, then a thirty-two-year-old farmer, and Patience Newton, a twenty-two-year-old house servant.[113]

Why did the Sizemore slaves take their former owner's surname upon emancipation? Of course I would like to believe it was because they had been relatively well treated. On the other hand, it may simply have seemed the expedient thing to do. We will probably never know.

But we do know this: they remained in Mecklenburg County for decades. Elsewhere across the South, many blacks walked off the plantations during their first year of freedom, clogging the roads to the nearest town or city. But they were the exception. Like the Sizemores, the overwhelming majority of freedmen stayed in the same rural areas where they and their forebears had lived in bondage—many on the same farms.

In late 1865, Freedmen's Bureau agents throughout the South made a major effort to persuade freedmen to sign labor contracts with local farmers, ensuring employment for the coming year. Daniel Sizemore, who like most freedmen was illiterate, affixed his "X" mark to one such agreement on December 29, 1865.

Along with six other freedmen, Daniel bound himself as a laborer on the farm of Anderson Overbey, a neighbor of my ancestor, the white Daniel Sizemore. As payment for their services, Overbey pledged to each freedman a share of the corn, wheat, tobacco, cotton, sorghum, peas, flax, oats, and brandy produced on the farm.

A week later, on January 5, 1866, the freedman Daniel Sizemore signed a supplemental contract with Overbey pledging the labor of "his wife Patience & three children, Henry, Dick & Ben" for the year and agreeing to let Overbey "manage and controle his wife and children." In return, Overbey agreed to "find Provisions to the said Daniel, wife and three children, and clothe his wife and three children with one summer suit and one winter suit of clothing and one pair of shoes each for the four."[114]

The child Ben was undoubtedly Uncle George's father.

In practical terms, life for the freedmen under such labor contracts was probably little different from life before emancipation. In some isolated pockets of the South, ex-slaves didn't even know they were free for as long as two years after the war. And as contracted laborers, many were plunged ever deeper into dependency and debt. The African-American scholar W.E.B. DuBois put it this way: "The white planter endeavored to keep the Negro at work for his own profit on terms that amounted to slavery and which were hardly distinguishable from it."[115]

Even on those terms, some planters reneged.George Graham, the Freedmen's Bureau superintendent in Mecklenburg County, wrote to his superiors in January 1868, "Many of the Planters that made contracts with the Freedmen for 1867 have failed to fulfill their part of the contracts and in fact in many cases have refused to settle with the Freedmen. . . . Very many of the Planters acted on the principle that as the Freedmen had no one to advise them, they (the Planters) would cheat them out of what they could."[116] Moreover, Graham reported, it was futile for freedmen to try to enforce their rights in the Mecklenburg courts. "The county courts of this county are but a political farce," he wrote. "As for justice to Freedmen, the thing will soon be unknown in the courts of this Division."[117]

It appears that one of my ancestors faced an allegation of failing to uphold his end of a labor agreement. In February 1867, Rhoda Pollard, a freedwoman, charged that a white man identified in Freedmen's Bureau records as Harble Sizemore refused to give her and her daughter Delia the clothing he had promised them in return for their labor. I suspect the defendant was actually Harvel Sizemore, the son of my slave-owning ancestor Daniel Sizemore who had been a Confederate reservist in the war. The bureau official who heard the case resolved it this way:

"Wrote him if he did not give up the articles I should see the law enforced."[118]

Despite such difficulties, bureau officials reported that the freedmen seemed disposed to work faithfully for rock-bottom wages while striving to improve their lot. In particular, the ex-slaves had a consuming hunger for education. One Virginia school official, trying to describe the freedmen's enthusiasm, said the phrase "*anxious* to learn" was insufficient: "They are *crazy* to learn."[119]

Booker T. Washington, born on a tobacco farm in Franklin County to the west of Mecklenburg, wrote later that his mother told him whites considered reading too dangerous for black people. "From that moment," he recalled, "I resolved that I should never be satisfied until I learned what this dangerous practice was like." He sometimes accompanied his master's daughter to the schoolhouse door, and the sight of the white children sitting in class made a profound impression. "I had the feeling," he wrote, "that to get into a schoolhouse and study in this way would be about the same as getting into paradise."[120] Washington, of course, went on to become one of the foremost educators of his age, working his way through what is now Hampton University and helping establish Tuskegee Institute in Alabama.

Back in Mecklenburg, the passion for learning burned no less brightly. "There is a great need of schools in this Division," Graham, the Freedmen's Bureau superintendent, wrote to headquarters. "The Freedmen offer to furnish the school rooms and fuel and lights but are not able to pay teachers."[121]

In February 1868, Graham wrote his superiors requesting that the bureau pay the transportation costs for a Miss Minnie Graham to come from Delaware County, New York, to open a freedmen's school in Mecklenburg. (It isn't clear from the correspondence, but Miss Graham might well have been a relative of Superintendent Graham.) The freedmen had offered to raise sufficient money to pay the teacher's board, Graham wrote.

"And Miss Graham proposes to come on those terms, viz. transportation and board. She is from one of the best families of my native county, highly educated and a first grade teacher of the free schools there; does not ask for pay, is willing to teach one term of six to eight months without compensation. I have applied to societies for teachers. They write that they have no means to send more teachers. I wrote to my friends; they cannot offer anyone, so this is the only chance I see for a school."[122]

The bureau agreed to pay Miss Graham's way to Virginia, and by the end of April, Superintendent Graham triumphantly reported that not one but two freedmen's schools were in operation: Graham's School of Clarksville and Andrews School of Boydton. By October, there were four.

Similar scenarios were playing out across the South. By 1870 there were more than four thousand schools under Freedmen's Bureau supervision educating nearly a quarter million pupils. Even so, only about one in ten black children were in school.[123] Most whites remained unalterably opposed to the idea of educating blacks, believing, as the scholar DuBois has written, that "learning will spoil the nigger for work."[124]

Miss Graham and the other Northern teachers who came south to teach in the freedmen's schools did so at some personal risk. In Alamance County, North Carolina, just over the state line from Mecklenburg, a crippled teacher was dragged out of his bed without his crutches by Ku Klux Klansmen on a cold November night, whipped with raw cowhide and left in the woods.[125] In parts of the Deep South, teachers were beaten, stabbed, and killed.

Meanwhile, Virginia and most other Southern states enacted "black codes" restricting freedmen's lives in various ways. The Virginia Vagrant Act of 1866 provided for the arrest of "vagrants"—basically, anyone who was unemployed—who were then hired out to employers granted the right, under some circumstances, to work them under ball and chain.[126]

Southern whites "knew one thing above all others, just as certainly as they knew that the sun rose and set," DuBois wrote, "and that was, that a Negro would not work without compulsion, and that slavery was his natural condition."[127]

That mindset has shown a stubborn persistence. In the years after emancipation, it simmered barely under the surface until it soon extinguished a brief, heady flowering of self-government by men who had so recently been considered chattel.

—5—

The Fragility of Freedom

When I studied American history in my segregated Southside Virginia high school, we skated lightly over the Reconstruction period. During the little time we spent on it, our teacher told us it was one of the most corrupt eras in American politics, a misguided—but mercifully brief—attempt to endow African-Americans with political power they weren't ready for.

That interpretation reflected the conventional wisdom of the day, advanced by a generation of Southern white historians. A striking example is *The Negro in Virginia Politics, 1865–1902,* by Richard Lee Morton, a longtime chairman of the history department at the College of William and Mary. Morton Hall, an academic building where I attended classes on the Williamsburg campus in the 1960s, is named in his honor. Originally published in 1918 as a doctoral dissertation, the book is shockingly racist by today's standards. It brands Reconstruction an "evil period" in which the freedmen were "but shortly removed from savagery and were utterly unfit for citizenship in a democracy."[128] "Politics," Morton wrote, "with its excitement, its conventions and speech-making, was very fascinating to these childlike people."[129]

The truth, however, is that the pioneering African-American officeholders of the Reconstruction era, fresh from the degradation of slavery, fostered some of the most progressive and enlightened legislation in American history. And they did it in the face of implacable opposition from their former masters. Theirs is a story of indomitable grit.

The Reconstruction Act of 1867 was enacted by the Radical Republican-led Congress over the veto of Lincoln's slave-owning successor in the White House, Andrew Johnson. The law put the Southern states under temporary military rule. In order to be readmitted to the Union, they were required to create new constitutions guaranteeing universal male suffrage and to ratify the Fourteenth Amendment to the Constitution granting the freedmen citizenship and equal protection under the law. The federal law disenfranchised former Confederates and gave freedmen the right to vote for delegates to constitutional conventions in each state. A look at voter turnout in the Virginia election of 1867 illustrates the freedmen's hunger for self-government. Statewide, 88 percent of registered African-Americans voted, compared to 63 percent of whites.[130]

Of the 105 delegates elected to the Virginia convention, a majority were Radical Republicans. Of those, twenty-five were African-American. Some were capable of soaring rhetoric. Willis Hodges, an African-American delegate from Princess Anne County, now part of Virginia Beach, described slaveholders' legacy in one of his early floor speeches: "They have trampled us down into the very dirt for centuries. They have made it unlawful for us to read, to preach, or in any way to elevate ourselves. They have kept us down with a brutal and a cruel hand. The degradation, the ignorance which they presume to despise in us, is all the work of their own hands."[131]

Thomas Bayne, an African-American delegate from Norfolk, spoke of how slavery degraded whites as well as blacks: "Every white man from Georgia to Maine, until the Emancipation Proclamation came to us, was an indirect slave. He was tied hand and foot to the dead body of slavery. The Proclamation of Emancipation came to us and set us all free."[132]

In the minority at the convention were members of the Conservative Party, which had been formed as a self-proclaimed "white man's party" dedicated to keeping Virginia's government "under the control of the white race." (The Conservatives later aligned with the national Democratic Party, which resisted the Radical Republicans' Reconstructionist agenda.) John Marye, a Conservative delegate from Spotsylvania County, reminded the convention that Jesus Christ lived amid slavery but never condemned it. "On the contrary," he said, "there came out of those blessed lips the recognition and the endorsement of that as a legitimate institution of Christian society."[133]

Jacob Liggett, a Conservative delegate from Rockingham County, admitted that slaves were whipped, but argued that their treatment was no worse than that meted out to European serfs. "The cow-hide and the lash did exist; and if it was a wrong, it was a wrong which grows out of the condition of every society," he said. "Society is not perfect, nor will it be perfect until a millennial dispensation shall arrive."[134]

Mecklenburg County sent two delegates to the convention, both Radical Republicans: John Watson, a freedman, and Sanford M. Dodge, a white preacher and distiller from New York. There, Dodge proposed a provision guaranteeing religious liberty to all Virginians. The constitution adopted in April 1868 included a section substantially similar to his proposal.

The press heaped unrelenting abuse on the freedmen and their political allies, the "carpetbaggers"—Northerners who came South after the war—and "scalawags"—Southern whites who joined the Republican cause. Editors described the convention with demeaning epithets such as "the Black Crook Convention."

Dodge, the "carpetbagger" delegate from Mecklenburg, was the target of one such attack in the *Richmond Enquirer*: "A few nights since, a man named Sanford M. Dodge, supposed to be a white man, a delegate from Mecklenburg county to the late Black Crook Convention, was seen by a gentleman of this city promenading one of the principal streets with a negro woman on either arm. Dodge is one of the lowest and filthiest of the carpet bag race, and we always had serious doubts whether he was a white man."[135]

The new constitution ensured freedom of speech and the press, prohibited slavery and secession, prescribed voting by secret ballot, established a 12 percent maximum interest rate on debts, and extended the elective franchise to all male citizens twenty-one and over, with certain exceptions. Those who had "engaged in insurrection or rebellion against the United States" would not be allowed to vote, and all those elected to office would be required to take an oath declaring that they had never borne arms against the Union.

One of the convention's most notable achievements was a requirement that the state establish a uniform system of free public schools—the first such law in Virginia history. "Public education for all at public expense was, in the South, a Negro idea," the scholar W.E.B. DuBois has written.[136] Some measures proposed but not adopted at the 1867–68 convention became law decades later and are now universally accepted, including female suffrage, racially integrated schools, and the eight-hour workday.

Unlike the more subtle forms of prejudice of our own time, the racism of the convention's minority delegates was naked and unapologetic. The minority report adopted by Conservative members of the Committee on the Elective Franchise and Qualifications for Office was brutally blunt in its assessment of the Virginia freedmen: "They have not the *intelligence* adequate to vote discreetly for the good of any class. They are descended, in direct line, from progenitors in Africa, who, since the flood, have held undisputed control of one of the most fertile continents of the globe, but have remained in such changeless and gross barbarism as to rank now, in the concurring judgment of mankind, lower in the scale of intellect and every moral attribute than the lowest type of the Caucasian race known to history, and quite as debased as any savage tribe yet discovered."

The Conservatives then had the audacity to cite the freedmen's previous servitude as a reason to deny them the rights enjoyed by whites: "Starting with this congenital weakness, the negroes of Virginia have, for two hundred years, lived under the depressing influence of constant slavery. If they had been moved by a desire for mental elevation, there were no adequate aids afforded for its attainment."

The inevitable result of granting equality to the freedmen, the Conservatives warned in apocalyptic prose, would be "that last and direst disaster which can befall the white race—the physical fusion and amalgamation of the races!"[137]

In an address to the people of Virginia published in the *Richmond Dispatch*, the minority Conservative delegates put on full display their abhorrence at the ex-slaves' rise to political power. "It is difficult to realize the situation which we have reached in the South," they wrote. "The mind is stupefied at the initiation of negro domination. It is a waking nightmare, whose horrible shadow cannot be pierced by the struggling faculties—a spell that neither the senses nor the reason can dissolve."[138]

The white press vilified the freedmen as ignorant, incompetent buffoons unfit to vote, let alone hold elected office. Across the South, many African-American officeholders were victims of violence, including murder.

One such incident occurred in May 1869 at Charlotte Court House, forty miles north of Daniel Sizemore's farm, when Joe Holmes was gunned down in broad daylight on the courthouse lawn. A freedman who worked as a shoemaker, Holmes had been a delegate to the constitutional convention. He was shot during a confrontation with a group of young white men. A coroner's jury determined that the killer was "some person unknown to the jury."

An account of the slaying in the *Richmond Dispatch* reflected the ridicule to which African-American politicians were subjected in the press, even in death: "The deceased was a prominent member of the late constitutional convention—prominent rather from the merriment he created on rising to speak than from any participation in the serious work of the body. . . . Joe's death will be regretted by all who knew him in the convention, and by those who have laughed over him in the 'Humors of Reconstruction,' where he figured as the 'great fire-eater.'"[139]

No one was ever prosecuted for Holmes' murder, but three local freedmen were hauled into court for speaking out about it. Among them were John Watson, one of Mecklenburg's delegates to the constitutional convention who was later elected to the Virginia House of Delegates, and Ross Hamilton, who succeeded Watson in the House. They were indicted and briefly jailed for conspiring to "incite the colored population of Charlotte to make war against the white population by acts of violence."[140]

* * * * *

On March 20, 1869, my ancestor Daniel Sizemore recorded his will, dividing his worldly possessions among his nine children. In 1860, his slaves had been valued at more than $11,000 altogether—the equivalent of $285,000 today, accounting for 85 percent of his wealth. Emancipation left him with just $1,500 in real estate and a few hundred dollars' worth of household goods.

The 1868 Virginia constitution was ratified by popular vote in July 1869, but the provisions barring ex-Confederate soldiers from voting or holding office—which were voted on separately— were defeated. In elections for the Virginia legislature, Radical Republicans won in majority-black counties like Mecklenburg, but Conservatives prevailed statewide. Virginia thus became the only Southern state to avoid a period of Radical Reconstruction.

As the 1870 election approached, the *Mecklenburg Herald,* a Conservative mouthpiece, offered this unsolicited advice to local freedmen: "We are the colored man's best friend—all he gets is from his own white people; if he has a shelter for his wife and children, he will get it from his own white people; if he has work for next year he must work Conservative land; if he has wood this winter it must be Conservative wood; if he gets any money for his labor he must get it from Conservatives. And we want the colored man too, he suits us best; the benefit is mutual, the difference is this however, we can do without the negro, for we can wait on ourselves, or hire white labor, or get Chinese, or make out in some way without the colored man, while he cannot live without us.

"So the colored man had better make friends with his own white people, and that quickly, for he has been losing ground every day since Lee's surrender, and as soon as he makes up with his own white people he can improve and do better if he will. But if he wants a war of races, he can have it, and we will drive him off Virginia soil before he is aware of it. Now, if you are in for a war of races vote against us, and do all you can to damage us, and we will understand you."[141]

Ridicule remained a favorite device of Southern editors. An account of the 1870 election in the *Herald*, while dripping with bemused derision, underlined the freedmen's passion for participation in the political process:

"The colored voters brought their last man to the front, and from the manner they besieged the ballot box, showed how much they appreciated the glorious privilege of putting in their votes. . . . The colored voters clung to their tickets when given them with a tenacity really amusing. We could not help thinking but some one had been singing to them –

> *It is a sin to steal a pin,*
> *A crime to cut a throat,*
> *But a plaguey sight bigger to stop a nigger*
> *From putting in his vote.*"[142]

Later that month, the *Herald* opined on the freedmen's proper place in the Mecklenburg economy: "Now we entertain no unkind feelings towards the colored man, far from it, he has our sympathy, but the kindness and good will should not be all on our part. As a laborer, when rightly controlled, he is in this country a general favorite, and in that capacity alone can he properly serve us. To be 'hewers of wood and drawers of water' is the inevitable doom of the race, and whenever they are led to believe otherwise they are led astray."[143]

The next week, the *Herald* agonized over the freedmen's continued electoral success in Mecklenburg and other counties of the "black belt": "The conflict of races has begun in earnest, the negro must yield to the supremacy of the white man, or he must be crushed out. . . . What! Shall old Mecklenburg county, with all her wealth, her intelligence, and her blood, be ruled and hectored over by a set of stupid negroes? . . . The response must come up from every true son of Mecklenburg and the Old Dominion, NO!"[144]

The *Herald* carried a dismissive account of a festive commemoration by local freedmen on the anniversary of Lee's surrender, April 9, 1871. Accompanied by drum, fife, banjo, and violin, some 250 celebrants marched around Boydton on foot and horseback before listening to several hours of speeches in front of the courthouse. One of the speakers was Ross Hamilton, a freedman who represented Mecklenburg in the Virginia House of Delegates.

"The animus of Ross' speech was to array class against class and tear open the old wounds," the editor snorted. "If we could get rid of politicians, there would be peace and quiet between the races."[145]

In another 1871 editorial, the *Herald* waxed nostalgic about the days of slavery and expressed doubts about whether Virginia's tobacco economy would be able to survive without it:

"It must be apparent to the minds of every thinking man that in the tobacco producing region of Virginia the character of the agriculture must radically change before the country can ever show any symptoms of returning prosperity. If we take the trouble to investigate the question of profits accruing from the culture of tobacco under the regime of slavery, it will be ascertained that had it not been for the peculiar increase of the 'peculiar institution,' or in other words, had not slavery bred slavery so rapidly, that the planters of Virginia long, long ago would have been forced to abandon its cultivation. It was certainly the most desirable crop for slave labor, because in its cultivation there was no leisure to impair the discipline, so necessary to keep them in a proper relation of subordination to their masters. Continuous labor, from the rising to the setting of the sun, from the beginning to the end of the year, was and is now indispensable to the culture of the fragrant weed.

"Tobacco culture was the only industry that could have ever kept slavery in its place in this part of Virginia. But slavery is gone, and, if we mistake not, the cultivation of tobacco must soon follow in its wake."[146]

Such predictions of tobacco's demise turned out to be premature, however. Virginia's Conservative-led government would find ways to circumvent the freedmen's hard-won new legal rights and reduce them to a subservient status that was not materially different from slavery.

The *Roanoke Valley*, another local newspaper, was full of indignation in 1872 when George W. Young, a Radical Republican "carpetbagger" from New Hampshire who served with Ross Hamilton in the statehouse, had the temerity to introduce a civil rights bill in that body. Young proposed "to require the landlords of hotels to seat negroes at his table aside of white gentlemen; to put them into beds to be occupied by white gentlemen; to give them the right to come into our pews and seat themselves amongst our families at church; in a word to enforce equality between the races," the editor complained. "There is little doubt, that when the bill comes up for consideration, it will promptly be kicked under the table."[147]

That prediction proved accurate: the legislation went nowhere. It would take nearly another one hundred years and an act of Congress before racial discrimination in public accommodations would become illegal.

The Fifteenth Amendment to the US Constitution, barring disfranchisement based on race, had been ratified in 1870. But once back in power, Virginia Conservatives began devising ingenious methods of limiting black voting power. The legislature enacted a poll tax as a prerequisite for voting and barred anyone convicted of petty larceny from the polls. The state also re-established whipping as a punishment for petty theft.[148]

In 1873, another Mecklenburg newspaper, the *Southside Virginian,* published an unapologetic justification for keeping black Virginians away from the polls and out of public office. "The Conservatives, acknowledging their legal, deny their moral right to represent the people as Governors, Senators, or other responsible officials, on the ground that they are unfitted to comprehend or discharge the duties," the editor proclaimed. "And, therefore, that the State may not be cursed with rulers, ignorant of the first principles of moral philosophy, unversed in the science of politics, and illiterate altogether, they oppose their elevation to these high and responsible offices."

The newspaper went on to heap scorn on Republican efforts to achieve social equality between the races: "What friendship is there in endeavoring to force upon society as equal, what society knows to be inferior, and how much reason is there in undertaking to force ignorance and culture, coarseness and refinement to commingle?"[149]

The Sizemore freedmen are a case study in the effectiveness of the poll tax in suppressing African-American voting. The one-dollar annual tax, levied on each voting-age male, was the equivalent of twenty-five dollars today. A list of Virginians who failed to pay the tax in 1881 tells the story. In Mecklenburg County, 83 percent of unpaid poll taxes were owed by African-Americans, including Daniel Sizemore, Ben Sizemore, Stephen Sizemore, Henry Sizemore, Booker Sizemore, Alex Sizemore, and Granderson Skipwith, the husband of my ancestor's former slave Alice Sizemore.[150]

* * * * *

For most of the South, Reconstruction essentially came to an end with the disputed 1876 presidential election, in which Democrat Samuel J. Tilden won the popular vote but Republican Rutherford B. Hayes was declared president by a special commission appointed by Congress. Hayes made it clear that he planned to put Reconstruction behind him and follow a policy of noninterference in Southern affairs.

The *Roanoke Valley* was jubilant as Hayes' intentions became clear: "In our section a cry of heartfelt anguish has ascended to Heaven itself for deliverance for years. Mr. Hayes becomes president, and holds out to us the olive branch, giving us all for which we asked."[151]

As it turned out, Virginia experienced one last gasp of Reconstruction-like policies during the four-year dominance of the Readjuster Party, named for its proposal to repudiate part of the state's war debt. The Readjusters swept to power in 1879, backed by an unlikely coalition of white farmers in the mountain counties and African-Americans in the "black belt." The orchestrator of that remarkable electoral feat was none other than William Mahone, the ex-Confederate general whose troops slaughtered hundreds of black Union soldiers in the Battle of the Crater.

Mahone, who weighed less than one hundred pounds, had a long gray beard and piercing eyes. His voice was thin and piping, almost a falsetto. He resettled from Clarksville to Petersburg after the war, was elected to the US Senate in 1879, and was Virginia's undisputed political boss for most of his six-year term. Under his guidance, the Readjusters repealed the poll tax, abolished the whipping post, poured money into the public schools, and established what became Virginia State University, the first fully state-supported, four-year institution of higher learning for blacks in America. [152] As a result of Mahone's patronage, growing numbers of African-Americans secured jobs as teachers, postal workers, clerks, policemen, and prison guards.[153]

In a newspaper interview after he left office, Mahone reflected on his dramatic odyssey from Confederate adulation as the "hero of the Crater" to vilification in the Conservative press as an "ogre" and a "devil" because of his support for biracial democracy. "I have stood upon Cemetery Hill and looked down on the scene of the great crater fight," he said, "and wondered in my heart if God could have any forgiveness for those men who led the South into that awful war, and are answerable for the blood, the misery, the ruin that followed. Yet under their teaching I was one of the most bitter and irreconcilable of all who flew to arms in the cause of the State and the Confederacy, and I never learned my wretched error, the awful blunder of the South, the curse of her institution of slavery and her traditions until I sat in the United States Senate, and day by day had borne in upon me the amazing significance of our form of government, what it meant, on what basis it was founded, how great and grand it was above any previous human effort, what it meant for humanity, and how much greater the nation was than any State."[154]

One of Mahone's key allies in the Virginia House of Delegates was Ross Hamilton, the Mecklenburg County freedman who had the longest tenure in the legislature of any African-American in the nineteenth century. A carpenter and storeowner in Boydton, Hamilton was described in a local society matron's memoirs as "a handsome mulatto." He was a staunch advocate for public education and voting rights and a fierce critic of the whipping post, which he denounced as a "relic of barbarism."[155]

Like most African-American officeholders of the era, Hamilton found public service to be no road to riches. In an 1885 letter to Mahone, he asked for a one-hundred-dollar loan to bury his eighteen-year-old daughter. "I have spent all the money I had trying to cure her," he wrote. "I would not call upon you to aid me, but my friends are poor."[156]

Hamilton was one of about one hundred African-Americans who served in the Virginia legislature between 1869 and 1890. Most were literate and owned property. Many were skilled tradesmen. One-third were born free. They introduced legislation to forbid discrimination in public transportation, protect tenants from abuse by landlords, ensure that blacks could serve on juries, and punish the perpetrators of lynchings.

Today they are virtually invisible in the history books.

From 1890 until 1967, not a single African-American served in the legislature. Even today, their numbers have never returned to the pinnacle they reached in 1869 at the dawn of Reconstruction.

* * * * *

The death knell for Virginia's attempt at biracial democracy sounded in Danville, fifty miles west of Clarksville, in November 1883.

Readjuster dominance of the state legislature had made it possible for African-Americans to gain control of the government in the majority-black town, drawing the enmity of whites. Seven of twelve town council members were black, as were four officers on the nine-person police force.

On Saturday, November 3, three days before Election Day, a fistfight broke out between a black man and a white man. The brawl turned into a full-fledged race riot, with blacks and whites shooting at each other. When the dust cleared, five blacks were dead and one white man mortally wounded.

"NEGRO RIOT," the headline in the *Richmond Dispatch* screamed the next day. "Bloodshed in the City of Danville . . . The Immediate Cause Negro Insolence."

"Every white man's blood has boiled when he read of the indignities to which the whites of Danville had for some time been subjected by the negroes there," the newspaper reported. "These negroes had evidently come to regard themselves as in some sort the rightful rulers of the town. They have been taught a lesson—a dear lesson."[157]

Democratic politicians seized on the violence, calling on white voters to unite against the danger of further black domination. The tactic worked. In that Tuesday's election, Democrats regained solid control of the legislature, launching a segregationist era that would hold sway in Virginia for nearly a century.

In the years following the Danville riot, Virginia descended with the rest of the South into a spiral of vigilante racial violence marked by periodic lynchings—mob executions of perceived criminals, almost always black. Contrary to a common public perception of lynchings as spontaneous eruptions of violence, they were often premeditated, even to the point of being announced ahead of time in the local newspaper. Many lynchings were celebratory public spectacles where cheering spectators could buy snacks from on-site food vendors. The grisly scenes were captured in photos and turned into postcards. Torture, mutilation, dismemberment, and burning of victims' bodies were common. Spectators collected the victims' body parts as souvenirs.

A 2017 compilation by the nonprofit Equal Justice Initiative counted more than four thousand lynchings in twelve Southern states between 1877 and 1950, with the largest numbers in the Deep South. Virginia had the fewest: eighty-four.[158] Two of those occurred in Mecklenburg County, although few details about the victims have survived: a man named Dick Walker in May 1886 and an unnamed victim in December 1890.[159]

In the eyes of many whites, one of the gravest crimes a black man could commit was sexual assault on a white woman. Lynchings of such offenders were widely excused if not praised.

Such was the case in Halifax County, just west of Clarksville, in July 1888, when a black man named Bruce Younger was lynched for attempted rape.[160] The *Danville Register* published this response: "Another brute has committed a fiendish act in Halifax county, and has paid the inevitable penalty of his crime. There is an unwritten law in this land of chivalry where woman is honored and revered and the penalty of its infraction is certain and ignominious death. It is useless to talk of reason and the majesty of the law when such crimes are committed. There are some crimes which are so revolting to humanity and which so thoroughly arouse the indignation of men, that they think they are doing society a service in ridding the world of the brutal and merciless villains. It's useless to argue the whys and wherefores, the unwritten law is fixed and its judgments are severe. Let the unrighteous beware of its violation."[161]

Just nine months later, in April 1889, another black man, Scott Bailey, was lynched in Halifax County for the same alleged crime.[162]

Interracial sex was such a taboo that little attention was paid to the question of consent. In Pittsylvania County outside Danville in 1892, George Towler, a black farmhand, was hanged by five white men for the alleged attempted rape of his employer's teenage daughter, even though it was well known locally that the two had been lovers for some time.[163]

The bloodiest peacetime incident of racial violence in Virginia history occurred in Roanoke, one hundred miles northwest of Clarksville, in September 1893. Thomas Smith, a black man, was charged with robbing and assaulting Mrs. Henry Bishop, a white woman who had come to town to sell produce from her family's farm. Smith was lodged in the city jail, where a crowd began to gather, and the Roanoke Light Infantry was called out.

The crowd soon became a howling mob of five thousand, angrily demanding that the prisoner be handed over. Men began to batter the jail door. Someone fired a gun and the militiamen returned fire, shooting into the crowd. When it was over, twelve men lay dead and twenty-one wounded, some mortally.[164]

Smith was spirited surreptitiously out a back entrance of the jail, but the mob caught up with him the next morning. Soon his bullet-riddled body was dangling at the end of a hemp rope tied to a hickory tree on a downtown street corner. Relic hunters stripped scraps of clothing off the body as souvenirs. Finally, amid deafening cries of "Take him and burn him!" the mutilated corpse was hauled by wagon to the riverside and burned on a pyre of cedar trees. The flames leapt twenty feet into the air, drawing frantic cheers from the mob. Smith's fifteen-year-old sister was among the witnesses.

Employing what by now was a well-worn phrase, a coroner's inquest found the lynching was carried out by "persons unknown to this jury."[165]

Periodic lynchings continued to occur in Virginia into the 1920s. The popularity of lynching prompted one black newspaper in 1911 to call it "the National Pastime."[166] Finally, at the urging of Louis Jaffe, editorial page editor of the *Virginian-Pilot*—where I later spent most of my career—the General Assembly passed a law in 1928 making lynching a state crime. Jaffe won a Pulitzer Prize for his advocacy.[167]

The great jazz singer Billie Holiday brought the horrors of lynching into American living rooms with her recording of the unsettling protest song "Strange Fruit" in 1939:

> *Southern trees bear a strange fruit*
> *Blood on the leaves, blood at the root*
> *Black bodies swinging in the Southern breeze*
> *Strange fruit hanging from the poplar trees*
> *Pastoral scene of the gallant South*
> *The bulging eyes and the twisted mouth*
> *Scent of magnolia sweet and fresh*
> *Then the sudden smell of burning flesh*

Here is a fruit for the crows to pluck
For the rain to gather, for the wind to suck
For the sun to rot, for the tree to drop
Here is a strange and bitter crop.[168]

* * * * *

William Mahone attempted a political comeback as the Republican nominee for governor in 1889. Once again, the Democrats played the race card, warning that a Mahone victory would return African-Americans to political power.

Nevertheless, Mahone stuck to his vision of biracial democracy, telling voters in a campaign brochure, "The colored man is here to stay. . . . His place cannot be supplied. He is in great measure the life-giving power to all our industrial pursuits. His labor contributes to the wealth of the State, and the more we enlarge his capabilities and stimulate his efforts the greater will be his contributions."[169]

Mahone carried Mecklenburg and other counties of the "black belt," but lost the election. He died in 1895 and was buried in Petersburg's Blandford Cemetery, not far from the scene of the carnage at the Crater.

In 1900, a convention was called to replace the 1868 state constitution. There was no attempt to conceal its purpose: the effective disfranchisement of African-American voters. The resulting constitution of 1902 resurrected the poll tax and erected still more barriers to the polls. Voting was restricted to males twenty-one and over who had paid the tax and either owned property or could read or understand and (in either case) explain a section of the constitution. Unlike the constitution of 1868, which was ratified by voters in a referendum, the new one was simply proclaimed the law of the state.

It had the desired effect. The size of Virginia's electorate was cut in half. African-American participation at the polls plummeted to a negligible level. Virginia had embarked on an era of slavery by another name.

Throughout the first half of the twentieth century, Virginia governors were typically elected by less than 10 percent of the state's adult population. Characterizing Virginia's political climate in 1949, political scientist V.O. Key Jr. wryly remarked that "by contrast Mississippi is a hotbed of democracy."[170]

With black Virginians effectively removed from the political process, Claude Swanson, the successful Democratic candidate for governor in 1905 and later a US senator, was able to declare, "We have no Negro problem here."[171]

The new constitution received a gloss of semiapologetic approval in the historian Richard Lee Morton's 1918 treatise on the Reconstruction era. "The negro had been a failure and a menace in politics. . . . Therefore he must be removed," Morton wrote. "It is a matter of regret that it has been necessary to disfranchise a large body of citizens by methods some of which did not seem in themselves commendable," but they "threatened to corrupt the whole body politic of the Commonwealth."[172]

Another historian, Ralph Clipman McDanel of the University of Richmond, was unqualified in his endorsement of the 1902 constitution in a 1928 book: "The Convention did the State a great service when it removed the negro from politics and thus rendered the purification of the electorate possible."[173]

For Virginia's African-Americans, the welcome mat had been pulled up and the door to the fruits of democracy slammed shut. As the new century dawned, thousands of them—including many of the black Sizemores of Mecklenburg County—began voting with their feet.

—*6*—

The Great Migration

On Christmas Day in 1879, Ben Sizemore—former child slave and contract laborer—married Mary Daniel. The bride and groom were both twenty-one.[174]

Christmas was a popular day for weddings among the Sizemore freedmen. It fell during a rare fallow season for the tobacco crop, and it was a day when the unceasing cadence of farm work slowed to a minimum.

Another Christmas Day wedding was that of Alice Sizemore, another of my ancestor's former slaves, to Granderson Skipwith in 1868.[175] That was before the veil of segregation fully split the South's churches. Thus, Alice and Granderson were married by the Reverend F.N. Whaley, the same minister who said the vows when my great-grandfather Thomas L. Sizemore married his bride Mary Catherine Gold in 1870.

Ben and Mary Daniel Sizemore are listed in the 1880 census as living next door to Samuel Daniel, a white farmer.[176] Their children—Uncle George's half-siblings—came in quick succession over the next ten years: Mary, Jordan, Minnie, Dodson, Ben Jr., and John.

"In those days, you were a big man if you had a big family," Uncle George told me. "My daddy was still having children when his children were having children."[177] Ben was a big man in the literal sense, too, even bigger than Uncle George—six feet six and 290 pounds.

In all likelihood, Ben and Mary were sharecroppers for much of their life together. Across the South, freedmen had a burning desire to own their own land, seeing it as the best pathway to true independence from their former owners. But the vast majority were unable to buy land. Most whites refused to sell or extend credit to them.

Ben Sizemore with his first family. Front from left: Minnie and Mary Lee; back from left: Ben Jr., John, Dodson, and Jordan.

Eventually, Ben Sizemore proved the exception to the rule. In 1903, Reuben Chandler, a white farmer, sold him a five-acre tract three miles west of Clarksville.[178] The transaction was likely rooted in a historical connection between the two families: Reuben Chandler's wife, Martha, was the daughter of Anderson Overbey, the farmer who had contracted for the labor of Daniel Sizemore's family, including eight-year-old Ben, in 1866.

Ben moved his family into a log cabin on his new land— but by 1910, he had become a widower. Four of his six children were out on their own by then, and he had taken in his widowed mother and two nieces, Josephine and Page, daughters of his brother Stephen.[179] There is no record of Stephen in Mecklenburg County after 1900. Uncle George doesn't know where he went, but he thinks he knows why he departed: "I was told my daddy had a good boss man, but Uncle Stephen's wasn't so good, so he left."

Ben married his second wife, Ella, in 1913, and the marriage produced five more children: Elsie, Esther, Flora, George, and Edna. In addition, the household included Ella's sons from her first marriage, Isaac and Piercie.

Ben was also able to expand his land holdings, thanks to the Reverend George W. Wharton. A true Renaissance man, Wharton was an 1880 graduate of Hampton Institute, now Hampton University. A mixed-race native of Virginia's Eastern Shore, he was one in a legion of young African-Americans schooled at Hampton who fanned out across the region to teach in black schools. He secured a teaching job at a one-room school in the Averett community five miles west of Clarksville and soon organized a Sunday school, out of which grew Beautiful Plain Baptist Church. He studied law for a year at Howard University and spent his vacations taking theology courses.

The Rev. George Wharton

He soon branched out into farming as well. "I . . . saw that if I stayed there, I must do something beside teaching," he wrote in *The Southern Workman,* a Hampton Institute maga-zine, in 1898. "I found I had to go to work just like any other man. It was humiliating at first, because the people thought that a teacher or a preacher ought to be above working with his hands, but . . . I believe that every preacher and every teacher ought to get down among the people, and work

with them. . . . The great need of the black man to-day is instruc-
tion in farming, for he has not had the opportunity to learn from
theory or practice. During the days of slavery he learned only how
to work, not how to farm."[180]

Wharton yearned to be a landowner, but for years he had to
be content with two small rented patches on which he labored
from 3:00 a.m. until school opened and from school closing until
9:00 p.m., working out the best agricultural methods for the local
soil and climate. Finally a white planter, out of admiration for his
perseverance, sold him seventy-two acres. He eventually acquired
more than three thousand acres, which he subdivided and sold to
black farmers in parcels of fifty to one hundred acres over long
terms with small payments. He also became the local postmaster
and operated a general store that sold farm supplies and fertilizer.
He drew up deeds, wills, and contracts for people in the community, often at no charge.[181]

In 1919, Wharton sold Ben and Ella Sizemore the sixty-four-
acre farm where Uncle George still lives today.[182]

"That man was something else," Uncle George told me. "He
was the smartest man in Mecklenburg County." Uncle George
was named for and baptized by him.

In an address to a regional Sunday school convention in 1909,
Wharton mused about how far his people had come:

"As you sit in this body today you occupy a station in the
world's history when contrasted with past conditions makes
you a peculiar people. Your ancestors were heathens, you are
Christians; your ancestors were property, you are property hold-
ers; your ancestors were ignorant, you are learned; your ancestors
were conquered, you are conquerors of the highest rank. The man
who conquers self is greater than he who takes a city. You have
opportunities which the white race have not. You belong to a race
which has made greater progress in the time you have been free
than any in the world's history. . . . The fate of this race of ours
will be the fate of us all."[183]

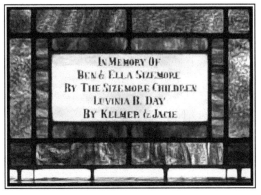

This stained glass window in Wharton Memorial Baptist Church honors Ben Sizemore and his second wife, Ella.

After his death in 1932, Wharton's church was renamed Wharton Memorial Baptist Church in his honor. Whenever the African-American Sizemores hold their family reunion in Clarksville, they gather en masse at the church for the Sunday service. Uncle George, a longtime member of the men's choir, still belts out solos in a booming baritone.

* * * * *

Based on the autosomal DNA test taken by Uncle George's niece Eugene, the family is descended from the Yoruba people on the "Slave Coast" of West Africa encompassing Togo, Benin, and western Nigeria. One of Africa's most artistic peoples, the Yoruba are noted for ritual performances honoring their ancestors, using masks and costumes made of richly colored and patterned cloths.

To this day, the African-American Sizemores still revere their elders. Uncle George, the last surviving member of his generation, is the unquestioned patriarch. At family reunions, they hang on his every word and make sure his plate is piled high with food and his iced-tea glass kept full. He receives the adulation with an easy grace and a twinkle in his eye.

"I'm one of the happiest people in the world," he once told me.

He comes by his good humor honestly. His father, who was widely known as Uncle Ben, was a happy man too, he recalled.

Uncle George remembers riding into town on a horse-drawn wagon beside his father, who would sometimes stop and treat himself to a nickel bag of peanuts. "I'd slip over beside him while he was driving and slip them out of his overalls pocket," Uncle George said. "When he caught me, I'd threaten to tell Mama he was spending money on peanuts." Thanks to that good-natured blackmail, the treat remained their secret.

Ben would also take the family in the wagon to visit his adult children and their families. Those visits still bring a smile to the face of Uncle George's niece Eugene. "He would always bring us candy, and he would kiss each one of us," she told me. "He was a sweet granddaddy."

Besides the everyday wagon, the family had a Sunday wagon for going to church, with fresh straw spread out in the back for the children to sit on. The horses were dressed out in fancy leather harnesses and bridles with tassels. "The horses knew it was Sunday as well as we did" and behaved accordingly, Uncle George said. "That was our Cadillac. Some folks rode to church on mules. We children laughed and called them po' folks." But the Sizemores had to pinch pennies too. When the children's shoes wore out, Ben repaired them himself, sewing in new leather with the strong thread used to tie up tobacco leaves for curing.

Ben died in 1931 when Uncle George was twelve, leaving his widow Ella to raise his second family alone. "I don't know how Mama made it," Uncle George said. Ella, a retired teacher, went back to work teaching night school in the wood-frame schoolhouse beside the church. Her students were adults seeking the literacy skills they had been denied as children. While she taught, Ella made sure Uncle George studied his lessons late into the night by the light of the fireplace.

After he finished seventh grade, his schooling was interrupted for two years because there was no high school for blacks in Clarksville. When West End High School was built, he resumed his education, graduated in West End's first class in 1939 and won a scholarship to a trade school in West Virginia.

Ben Sizemore's second family. From left, Elsie Sizemore, Dixie Day, Edna Sizemore, Piercie Day, Esther Sizemore, and Uncle George Sizemore. The Day brothers were George's half-brothers on his mother's side.

As young men, Uncle George and his half-brother Piercie got jobs in a textile mill in Gibsonville, North Carolina, seventy-five miles from Clarksville, commuting daily from the farm. After working an eight-hour shift, they came home and plowed the fields in turn—Piercie until midnight and Uncle George until daybreak.

The rest of the Sizemore children, boys and girls alike, were also put to work in the fields at a young age.

Land ownership remained a largely unattainable goal for African-Americans in Mecklenburg County, and most of Uncle George's siblings ended up sharecropping. Raising tobacco, the staple crop, was a backbreaking, nearly year-round endeavor. Beginning in early February, the tiny seeds were planted in plant beds, protected from the cold by a gauze cover. In early May, when the young plants were four to five inches high, they were transplanted into fields that had been plowed with mules. The plants required constant attention: the flowers that sprouted at the top of the stalk were cut off to push the nicotine out into the leaves. "Suckers," small branches that sprouted along the stem, were stripped off. Tobacco worms—big green creatures as thick as a finger—had to be pulled off by hand and killed.

Harvest began in mid-July. The mature leaves were pulled off, tied together on sticks and hung from the rafters in log barns where they were cured over a wood fire. In the fall, the crop was hauled to town on wagons and sold in cavernous warehouses. The cloyingly sweet odor of the golden leaves wafted out the doors and permeated the air for blocks.

As the Sizemore children grew up, the US Supreme Court, in its 1896 *Plessy v. Ferguson* decision, validated Louisiana's railroad segregation law, opening the way for segregation of virtually all aspects of Southern life. Virginia joined the rest of the South in passing Jim Crow laws that circumscribed African-Americans' lives at every turn.

Above all, white segregationists were motivated by an all-consuming fear of racial amalgamation. Walter Scott Copeland, longtime editor of the Newport News *Daily Press*, wrote in 1925 that rather than submit to racial mixing, he "would prefer that every white child in the United States were sterilized and the Anglo-Saxon race left to perish in its purity."[184]

Tucked away somewhere in my attic is a box of handsome plaques won by the *Clarksville Times* in the 1970s. For decades, the plaques were given to the winners of the Virginia Press Association's annual award for journalistic integrity and community service—named the Copeland Award in honor of the Newport News editor. Embarrassed newspaper executives finally renamed the award in 2000 after researching Copeland's racist history.

Copeland was a vigorous booster of the Public Assemblages Act of 1926, which mandated separation of the races in all public places. Under this law, African-Americans were barred from hotels, restaurants, and other public accommodations. "When we traveled, we had to carry our own food," Uncle George told me. They went to segregated, substandard schools. Poll taxes and literacy tests kept them from voting. They had to use separate water fountains and restrooms. Doctors' waiting rooms were segregated. And in 1930, the Association for the Preservation of Virginia Antiquities even barred black Virginians from visiting historic Jamestown Island, where their first African forebears arrived in 1619.[185]

Like most African-Americans of his era, Uncle George said, he was schooled to always keep his guard up when dealing with white people, lest he be perceived as uppity. "My mother always used to tell us to be careful when we went out—to watch what you do and what you say," he told me.

Uncle George remembers many bus rides when he and his kin were relegated to the back of the bus, closest to the exhaust fumes. On trains, the arrangement was just the opposite: blacks were herded into the front car, which got the most coal smoke from the steam engine.

Occasionally, the system could be circumvented with a bit of ingenuity. Two of Uncle George's sisters, Elsie and Flora, were deaf-mutes who attended a special school in Newport News. Uncle George remembers one trip with his sisters to visit kin in New York when the family, famished and having eaten all the food they brought from home, stopped at a restaurant with a "whites only" sign. When they were told they wouldn't be served, Uncle George pulled out a slip of paper and wrote a note saying they were all deaf. The proprietor finally relented and served them.

"They talked about us like we were dogs, but we got a good meal," he said.

For someone whose life spanned some of the darkest times of deprivation in African-American history, Uncle George is remarkably free of bitterness. He would rather talk about the gains African-Americans have made than what they were denied.

"We came a long ways in a hurry," he told me once. "We have everything, and people are complaining. We used to have nothing, and people were happy. Sometimes I think we had too much too quick." His perspective might not sit too well with younger generations of African-Americans, but I think it reflects the long arc of improvement, however halting, that Uncle George has seen over his long life.

That said, he is not blind to the pathologies that afflict African-American life today, such as the disproportionate incarceration of young black men in the nation's prisons. "What bothers me most," he said, "is boys not going to school—going to jail instead."

* * * * *

The indignities of Jim Crow, the lack of economic opportunity and the ever-present fear of racial violence propelled a mass exodus of six million African-Americans from the South to the North during the first half of the twentieth century. Over the decades, most of Mecklenburg's black Sizemores joined what has come to be known as the Great Migration.

The first in Uncle George's family to head north was his half-brother Ben Sizemore Jr., who went to New Jersey between 1910 and 1920, before Uncle George was born. The two siblings never met.

"Daddy said Ben Jr. didn't like farm life, and he didn't like working for white people—I'll just say it plain," Uncle George told me.

Ben Jr. found work as a laborer in an oilcloth factory in Passaic.[186] He died at age forty-two in 1931, the same year as his father. Uncle George's cousins Josephine and Page, who lived with the family for several years as children, also went to New Jersey before 1920, finding employment as live-in maids for white families.[187]

The Great Depression of the early 1930s spurred another wave of northward migration. In 1932 Uncle George's sister Esther went to Boston, where she, too, found a job as a domestic worker. Like others who went north, she sent any extra money she made back home to her Virginia family.

Page (left) and Josephine Sizemore, Uncle George's cousins, lived with his family for a time until they moved to New Jersey to find work between 1910 and 1920.

"That's how we saved our place," Uncle George told me. His widowed mother had fallen behind in payments on the farm, and it was put up for public auction by the bank. The extra money from Esther helped stave off foreclosure at the last minute. Another time, the family sold a pig to make that month's payment.

Uncle George's nephew Bill was the next to migrate, landing a job as chauffeur to the owner of a clothing store in New Haven, Connecticut, in the mid-1930s. His wife, Ruby, became the white family's cook. Over the next few years, Bill and Ruby's house at 491 East Street in New Haven became a gateway for Mecklenburg Sizemores making the northward trek. One by one, Bill's siblings—Rose, Mozelle, Mary, Sam—moved in with their brother until they could find places of their own.

I learned the story of Bill, who shares my name, from his son Howard, who shares my father's name. Those are only two of several coincidental echoes between the white and black Sizemore family trees. Living in our segregated worlds, none of us knew about our namesakes until I began researching this book.

Howard stayed with his grandmother in Virginia until he turned six in 1940, when his parents sent for him. He has lived in Connecticut ever since. "I would consider myself a Yankee," he told me.[188]

He is just one of many Yankees in the family. One of Uncle George's classmates in West End High School's first graduating class was his niece Minnie. Shortly after World War II, she moved in with relatives in Brooklyn, New York.

Howard Sizemore

"I got tired of working on the farm, and there were no other jobs," she told me. "Black folks couldn't work in stores or banks. And there was no money for college."[189] Instead, she got a factory job making handkerchiefs and aprons. Her husband, Roy Arnold, a subway conductor, died in his mid-forties.

Minnie ultimately retired from an office job with the New York City Board of Education. Since the mid-1950s, she and her son Ozzie have lived in the same small apartment in a mid-rise public housing complex in the Brownsville neighborhood of Brooklyn, where boxer Mike Tyson grew up. I visited them there on a brilliant fall day in 2013, when Minnie was ninety-three. Kids played noisily in the brick courtyard below, in the shadow of a century-old public school.

"It used to be nice when we first moved here," Minnie told me. "Now there's a lot of robbing and shooting."

Uncle George's nephew John was among the last of the Mecklenburg Sizemores to go north. In 1951, when he was just twelve, his mother died and he moved to New Haven, where he was raised by his older brother Sam.

John Sizemore

I visited John in the bright sunroom of his white two-story house in a leafy New Haven neighborhood shortly after my visit with Minnie. He told me that in Mecklenburg, he had toiled in the tobacco fields almost from the time he learned to walk. He attended a segregated one-room schoolhouse where a single teacher was responsible for six grades.

New Haven "was like a different world," he told me. He went to an integrated school and earned money from two paper routes. In the summers he worked in the clubhouse at a country club, pocketing big tips shining golfers' shoes. He attended Delaware State University on a football scholarship and worked as a middle-school teacher in New Haven for thirty-five years. Retired now, he has lost both legs to diabetes. He still keeps close ties to his family in Virginia. But he has no regrets about moving north.

"It turned out for the best," he said. "If I'd stayed, I wouldn't have had the same opportunities."[190]

Uncle George, on the other hand, never wanted to live anyplace but Mecklenburg County. The longest he ever stayed away was the nearly four years he spent in the Army during World War II. He was stationed in England and deployed to France on the fourth day of the Normandy invasion with an all-black firefighting battalion. The black soldiers' job was to put out the fires ignited by German "buzz bombs," an early type of cruise missile.

"It was the worst time of my life," he told me. "We lost a lot of people. It's something I'd like to forget. I don't talk about it much."

After the war, he paid a visit to his three sisters in New York, who helped him get a job there as a shipping clerk. "But I didn't like New York," he said. "I'm not a city boy." He soon quit and headed back to Mecklenburg, where he worked briefly in a textile mill. But he soon decided that wasn't for him, either. "I noticed all the black guys were working in the dye room," he said—slogging through who-knew-what toxins in rubber boots. So he left and spent the next thirty-four years working construction jobs. "I loved construction work," he said. "You

Uncle George Sizemore served in an all-black firefighting battalion in Normandy after the D-day invasion in 1944. / Clarksville Regional Museum

build something, and then you can go back and take a look at it."

Even for many of his kinfolk who went north, Virginia still feels like home. Several have told me they hope to retire there. One of those was Uncle George's great-nephew Jesse Austin, a resident of the Washington, DC, area, whom I met at the 2013 family reunion.

The Sizemore reunions are joyous, raucous gatherings set to a cacophonous soundtrack of regional accents ranging from the laid-back Southside Virginia drawl to the clipped cadences of New Jersey, Brooklyn, New Haven, and Boston. In contrast to my family's annual reunion—a single potluck supper—the African-American Sizemores put on a three-day affair featuring a fancy-dress banquet, a cookout, T-shirts, and gift bags.

"This is better than Christmas," Jesse told me, reveling in the glow of family love.[191]

Uncle George Sizemore at age 26 in 1946, just back from World War II.

The idea for the annual reunion germinated when a couple of the Northern Sizemores paid a visit to Uncle George's niece Eugene Watkins and her daughter Evella in Clarksville. "I said, 'We don't know half of our family. We need to get together,'" Evella recalled. At the first reunion, held at Eugene's house in 1983, Sizemores showed up from all over the country, many of them meeting for the first time. As a DJ played soul records, they picnicked on the lawn and stayed up late into the night getting to know each other.

Minnie Arnold, the retiree who has spent most of her life in Brooklyn, told me she sometimes wishes she had moved back to Virginia after her husband died. Life on the farm in Mecklenburg was hard, but "it was a happy life," Minnie told me. "We had no money, but we had food to eat. We raised our own. When I came to New York, I was shocked to see people in soup lines." For years, she kept up with Clarksville happenings by subscribing to the same local newspaper I once edited. I remember seeing her name on the mailing list, when I was still blissfully ignorant of our century-old family ties.

Minnie told me she has a recurring daydream about her ancestral home.

"When I win the lottery, I'd like to build a hotel in Clarksville—the Sizemore Hotel," she said. "Everybody could stay there during our reunions. Wouldn't that be nice?"

—7—

Rose and Charles

When Rose Shealy joined the Great Migration in 1935, it was for all the usual reasons. She chafed under the strictures of Jim Crow. She didn't care for farm life and yearned for more economic opportunity. But in her case, there was another reason, perhaps most compelling of all: she was an unwed teenage mother.

Rose's life story is a case study in one of slavery's most debilitating legacies: the fracturing of the family bonds that have held humankind together for millennia. I learned the story on a Sunday afternoon visit to the nursing home where she lived in South Boston, Massachusetts, in 2013. She was ninety-six at the time, and had been blind for twenty-five years. Sitting in a chair beside her bed, resplendent in a blue checked blouse and gold necklace, she talked about her life with disarming candor in a convivial conversation with me and her granddaughters Sandra Morris and Debra Morris Covington, and Debra's husband Paul.

Rose was born "out in the sticks," as she put it, on the Mecklenburg County tobacco farm where her father, Dodson Sizemore—the fourth child from Ben Sizemore's first marriage— was a sharecropper. She got pregnant at fifteen. What happened after the birth of her daughter sounds in the telling something like a banishment.

"Girlfriends I knew, two of them, the same thing had happened to them as happened to me," Rose told me. "When you get pregnant in Virginia, you're disgraced. And they talk about you, and nobody has nothing nice to say about you. And so the best way to do, we decided, was to leave.

"These girls moved to Massachusetts. They came home for the summer, and I followed them up here."[192]

Rose Sizemore Shealy (red shirt, second from left in the back row) is shown in this 1960s photo with her siblings: Erna (kneeling in front); Mary Lizzie and Mozelle (second row, from left); Charles, William, and John (back row, from left).

The three friends boarded a northbound bus in Clarksville, which at the time seemed like the big city to Rose. After eighty years, she still remembered being dazzled by all the lights as the bus rolled through New York City.

Like her friends, Rose found a job as a domestic worker in a white household. "Girls, even if they were educated, if they were black, they couldn't find good jobs," she said. "You took whatever you could get—cleaning and washing and ironing and taking care of babies. When I first come here, I got a job taking care of a little Jewish baby over near Boston College. That was my first job. I was getting seven dollars a week. That was big money.

"I didn't finish school. . . . You see, when you get pregnant they throw you out of school and you can't make no kind of life for yourself. . . . To think of it after I got older, that was kind of cruel. A fifteen-year-old girl! And they don't blame the man, you know. They just blame the woman."

Leaving her daughter, Willa, in Virginia to be raised by her grandfather, Rose had a series of domestic jobs in the Boston area before landing on the assembly line making rubber boots in a B.F. Goodrich factory in Watertown. Her marriage to Wheeler Shealy ended after sixteen years, and she retired on disability after twenty-seven years at Goodrich when glaucoma began to take her vision away in 1969.

I asked Rose if she ever missed Virginia after moving north.

"Never!" was her quick response.

"So life was better up here, was it?" I asked.

"Much better. People were much nicer. No Jim Crow."

"But there was still racism, wasn't there?"

"There will always be," she said. "I hate to say that, but it's going to last, I imagine, until everybody's dead."

I said I'd like to think bigotry would eventually fade away.

"Could be," Rose said. "Because the younger people these days are not as prejudiced, white and black. They enjoy each other's company, and they're not ashamed to be with each other. And there's more marrying between white and black now."

I agreed that if there's any hope of ending racism, it rests with the younger generation. Then Rose made it personal: "What would you say if your daughter brought home a black man?"

If it's someone she loves and who loves her and will treat her right, it wouldn't make any difference to me what color he was, I replied.

"Well, that's good. We got that all settled!" Rose declared with finality as the room erupted in laughter.

*   *   *   *   *

Several scholars have written about how slavery contributed to the disintegration of African-American family life. Nuclear households were difficult to achieve because of the predominance of "abroad" marriages—unions in which the man and woman did not live together.

The reasons for that were many. Virginia law mandated that slave children take the status of their mother. Often there was no acknowledgment of the father's role. The familial authority that would otherwise have been assumed by slave fathers was usurped by their children's white masters. At least one scholar has suggested that male slaves resisted marrying women on the same plantation because they couldn't bear to see their wives flogged or sexually abused.[193]

Work requirements frequently dictated that families be separated. Often, they were dispersed at the owner's death. Moreover, slave women's reproductive capacity was leveraged by their owners for their economic benefit, with no consideration of the impact on slave family life. W.E.B. DuBois put it this way:

"Sexual chaos arose from economic motives. The deliberate breeding of a strong, big field-hand stock could be carried out by selecting proper males, and giving them the run of the likeliest females. This in many Border States became a regular policy and fed the slave trade. Child-bearing was a profitable occupation, which received every possible encouragement, and there was not only no bar to illegitimacy, but an actual premium put upon it."[194]

Still, slaves clung to whatever family ties they could maintain, partly as a survival mechanism in a brutal system. Perhaps the greatest fear of slaves in Virginia and other border states was of one or more family members being sold to slave traders and shipped to plantations in the Deep South.

Most of those who were sold south never managed to reconnect with their families. One poignant example is Jennie Brown of Corinth, Mississippi, who wrote a plaintive letter to the sheriff of Mecklenburg County in 1882, two decades after emancipation: ". . . Please, inquiring of a family by the name of King. I was sold before the war by the sheriff. . . ."[195]

There is no record of any reply.

* * * * *

One of the most memorable people I met at the first African-American Sizemore reunion I attended, in 2011, was Charles Sizemore.

Like many of his kinsmen, Charles was big and barrel-chested, towering over me by half a foot, with a ready smile and an iron grip of a handshake. At six feet three inches and 257 pounds, he was well suited to the Sizemore name, he told me. "I fit the bill," he said. "I'm a size more!"

Charles Sizemore

Born in 1940, Charles had retired after a double career as a teacher and preacher. Fittingly, at that 2011 reunion, he was the guest preacher at the Sunday service at Wharton Memorial Baptist Church. In addition to being a talented sermonizer, he also displayed great skill as a pianist, accompanying and directing the men's choir in a rousing performance of gospel music.

After that reunion, Charles and I became good friends, meeting periodically for breakfast, lunch, or coffee near his home in Chesapeake, Virginia. Occasionally we encountered former students who remembered him fondly from his long career at Truitt Intermediate School, where he was once named Teacher of the Year. He always got a kick out of introducing me as his "cousin" and watching for the quizzical looks that played across people's faces as they surveyed our contrasting skin tones. He never failed to say a Christian blessing before we ate. When we parted, it was his policy to never say goodbye. It was always "See you later."

He always seemed happy. Only gradually did I come to realize that underneath a gloss of comfortable self-confidence, Charles was wracked by personal demons of despair and self-doubt, all rooted in his past.

Orphaned at birth, Charles grew up a ward of the state in Boston, passing through seven foster homes in fifteen years. He still bore emotional scars from the abuse he suffered. There were physical scars, too. In one home, his foster mother's adult son, who lived downstairs, regularly whipped him for the smallest infractions.

"There were times I worried I'd turn out to be the same kind of man," he told me. "But something internal kept me from going that way."

Charles repeatedly ran away from his foster homes, spending his nights wandering the streets of Boston and sleeping in doorways. "Boston was a cold, cruel place," he said, rife with racial prejudice. "We knew to stay in our neighborhood. You didn't go to the Irish section, unless you wanted to practice fighting."

Charles was a good student, but faced cruel taunts from classmates who ridiculed his secondhand clothes. He remembered lying awake at night after the annual awards ceremony in junior high school, wishing he had parents to see him receive his awards.

Upon graduation from high school in 1959, he joined the Navy, where he encountered more disappointment. Like many African-American recruits in that era, he was steered into duty as a steward, serving meals in the officers' wardroom. He resented his subservient role, but remained in it for his entire hitch. The last straw came after the assassination of President John F. Kennedy in 1963, when a lieutenant from Mississippi gloated over dinner, within earshot of Charles, "Serves that nigger-lover right."

"I thought, 'Maybe the Navy isn't the place for me. I'm smarter than that guy. Maybe I ought to go to college,'" Charles said. "So I got out."

He enrolled in San Francisco State University, where his path took a startling, life-altering turn: A young woman he met there was struck by his last name. She had an aunt back east who was married to a man named Sizemore, she told Charles. It's not a common name. Could there be a connection?

A few phone calls led Charles to the revelation that had eluded him for thirty years: his mother was Rose Sizemore Shealy.

As soon as he could, Charles went to Boston, where he met Rose and learned the story she had kept from the entire family: His father was an unknown sailor she had met five years after leaving Virginia. She couldn't keep Charles and retain her live-in housekeeping job, and she couldn't burden her father back in Virginia, who was already raising her daughter, with another child. So she gave him up.

Since discovering his roots, Charles struggled to establish the family ties that he always longed for. It was not always easy. His mother was always apologetic about giving him up, he told me. "I would tell her, 'Stop. You gave me the one thing I needed: life.'

"She really doesn't know me. She just knows what I've presented to her in the last forty years."

Charles began attending the Sizemore reunions in the 1990s, grasping eagerly for the love he felt there. "Uncle George helped me see that I really am a Sizemore, even though I didn't grow up with them," he said.

But he still felt a void.

"Everything I got, I got through trial and error," he said. "No one taught me how to be a real man, a good husband, a good father."

Charles' own family—four daughters, seven grandchildren, and three great-grandchildren—is scattered from Philadelphia to Atlanta to the West Coast. "I have four grandkids I've never been able to hold," he said. "They know *of* me, but they don't *know* me."

Charles and his third wife, Judy, faced financial struggles as well. He lost the pastorate he had held for nearly thirty years when the parishioners decided they wanted a younger minister. He and Judy bought a house, but lost it to foreclosure in the real estate crash of 2008. He felt he had failed his wife by not being able to give her financial security.

When I met Charles, he and Judy lived in a rented townhouse in a gritty section of Chesapeake where he presided over funerals of young African-American men he taught in middle school, victims of the urban violence that forms the dreary backdrop in cities across America. In his later years he was hobbled by health problems, including glaucoma and congestive heart failure.

"I try to keep smiling, but I feel like I'm in quicksand," he told me. "Desperation sometimes settles in. Sometimes I think, *What would I be like if I had had a mom and dad?* Then I put it out of my mind. There's no use worrying about it. . . . You win some, you lose some, you wipe your tears away. You cover your pain with laughter.

"I just wanted to be loved."

* * * * *

During my visit with Rose Shealy, I asked her what it was like being reunited with the son she hadn't known for thirty years. Her reply was tinged with ambivalence.

"I was kind of glad in a way, and then in another way I didn't care," she said. "I didn't have that real motherly love that I should have had. . . . He always wanted sympathy, because he didn't have no father. He didn't have no family. He missed family. For a while he used to use it—you know, like—'Pity me.' . . . Finally he got on your nerves."

Rose's daughter Willa—Charles' sister—died at seventy-two in 2007 after a hardscrabble life as a drug dealer and heroin addict. She had nine children, some of whom went down the same path.

"She did the best she could," her daughter Debra told me. "Charles and my mom both had abandonment issues." Debra and her siblings were largely raised by their great-aunt Mozelle, who lived nearby in Boston.

"When I was young I said I'd never be like my mother, but I was," Debra said. "It's a cycle. My grandmother never learned to nurture, and neither did my mother, and neither did me and my siblings."

Then she added a hopeful note: "I believe the cycle has broken with our kids. They're taking care of their kids."

But Debra's hopes were dashed in February 2016 when her three-year-old grandson Kenai Whyte died in a Boston hospital, the apparent victim of a severe beating. His twenty-three-year-old stepmother, the wife of Debra's son, was charged with second-degree murder in the case.

Debra Morris Covington, Rose Shealy's granddaughter, was devastated by the death in 2016 of her grandson Kenai Whyte, an apparent victim of child abuse.

I have a vivid memory of the rambunctious toddler. Debra had always made it a point to bring her grandchildren to the Sizemore reunions, hoping they would absorb some of the love and warmth that are always in abundance there. But little Kenai's fate demonstrates that the cycle of family dysfunction is distressingly hard to break.

When I spoke with Debra a year after her grandson's death, she was still disconsolate. "He was my baby," she said. Compounding the tragedy of his death, Debra's relationship with her son was fractured as well. And an ensuing custody battle sharply limited her contact with her surviving grandchild, a girl, to one hour a month. "In a way, I lost them all—my son, grandson and granddaughter," she said. "It's overwhelming."

* * * * *

Rose Sizemore Shealy died three days after Christmas in 2013, less than four months after I met her. None of her Virginia kin—including Charles, who had been in and out of the hospital that fall—braved the frigid temperatures to make the trip to Boston for the funeral.

Charles' youngest daughter Thylon read the eulogy he wrote for his mother.

Charles chose a verse from the Bible, Revelations 20:12, for his text: "And I saw the dead, small and great, standing before God, and books were opened. And another book was opened, which is the Book of Life. And the dead were judged according to their works, by the things that were written in the books."

The books about Rose's life would contain chapters from all of her relatives and friends, Charles wrote. "My chapter may have questions yet unanswered, thoughts yet unspoken. . . . It would also include how she loved her children in spite of some very difficult actions when she was younger. . . . But believe it or not, all of the chapters in those books mean nothing to Rose, for she lived to have her name in the most important book in circulation. And everyone here will believe without a shadow of a doubt that she has made the transition from the earthly chapters and has entered into receiving an invitation to a place where there will be no more sickness, nor death. A place where the wicked will cease from troubling and the weary will be at rest. . . . I will see her again, and guess what: I see her beautiful face even now because our loved ones never really die in our minds. So be encouraged: God will wipe all tears from our eyes."

Their relationship was complicated, Charles told me later, but "I know she loved me in her own way."

Three years after he lost his mother, Charles' multiple health problems caught up with him. He died in February 2017 at seventy-six.

The last time I saw him, a couple of months before his death, he seemed to sense that his time was growing short. He told me, "I don't fear death. I'm okay, because this is not my home. I'm just passing through."

He asked me to promise to tell his life story so that others might learn from it. "I want them to know you need an inner peace," he said. "I always used to worry about what other people thought of me. My attitude now is, take me for who I am."

After he died, his wife asked me to say a few words at his funeral, an ebullient three-hour mashup of singing, shouting and preaching at a Chesapeake megachurch. I was happy to oblige.

"It's not just a coincidence that Charles and I had the same last name," I told the crowd. "Our families have a historical connection dating back to the pre-Civil War era. You can probably guess what the nature of that connection was." At that, a wave of knowing laughter rippled through the sea of black faces.

I briefly recounted the near-miraculous story of how Charles discovered his family roots. "Maybe more than most of us, because of his history I think Charles understood at a deep level how precious family ties can be," I said.

"He was an inspiration. He left the world a better place. It was a privilege to know him."

—8—

Daffodil and Me

Looking back on my youth in Southside Virginia in the 1950s and 1960s, I can count on one hand the opportunities I had to interact with African-Americans.

In South Boston, the small town in Halifax County where I spent my childhood, my parents employed a series of black women as maids. The term for such workers in my parents' social circle was "colored woman"—as in "My colored woman comes in on Tuesdays and Thursdays." I never heard my parents use the N-word. They were too genteel for that.

Then there was Charlie Williams, the kindly man who delivered groceries to the house from the small store he ran across town and who always had a lollypop or stick of bubble gum in his pocket for me. And in the summer, black children showed up at our door selling fresh blackberries they had picked in the wild.

Those pleasant memories aside, my perception of African-Americans was filtered through societal prisms of stereotype and ridicule. My father once took me to a minstrel show at the local high school in which white men in blackface indulged in exaggerated caricatures for laughs. I was too young to understand the racist mindset behind such a display, but looking back on it today makes me cringe.

In May 1954, a year before I started first grade, the US Supreme Court ruled in the landmark case *Brown v. Board of Education* that racially segregated public schools were unconstitutional. Many years later I learned that one of the authors of the supporting brief filed by US Attorney General Herbert Brownell in the case was William J. Lamont, a young Justice Department lawyer from Iowa and the father of my future bride, Mary Kay.

The high court directed in *Brown* that the schools be integrated with "all deliberate speed." But it would be more than a decade before Virginia fully complied. Well into high school, my classes continued to be lily white.

US Senator Harry Byrd, a descendant of the colonial-era William Byrd family and longtime boss of the segregationist political organization that controlled Virginia's government, declared that the *Brown* ruling created a "crisis of the first magnitude" and urged "massive resistance" to school integration.[196] Among Byrd's closest confidants—and one of the key architects and staunchest advocates of Massive Resistance—was Bill Tuck, Virginia's governor in the late 1940s and later a US congressman. Tuck was a Falstaffian, cigar-chomping, bourbon-swilling country lawyer who grew up in Halifax County near my father's family. My grandfather's general store served as the neighborhood polling place, and Tuck was a frequent visitor, especially on election days when local farmers would congregate to cast their votes into a weathered wooden ballot box under a towering oak tree. In 1949, during his governorship, Tuck was one of the guests at my grandparents' golden wedding anniversary.

In a 1955 speech in Halifax, Tuck made it crystal clear where he stood on the *Brown* decision: "I intend to resist with all the might I have this effort to distort the minds, to pollute the education, and to defile and make putrid the pure Anglo-Saxon blood that courses through the innocent veins of our helpless children."[197] In another speech, Tuck said integrated schools would lead to a "merger of the races" which would ultimately result in a "hybridized human, if human it would be."[198]

In 1958, Governor Lindsay Almond closed schools in Charlottesville, Norfolk, and Warren County rather than let them be integrated, locking nearly thirteen thousand pupils out of their classrooms. The state offered publicly funded tuition grants to white parents who enrolled their children in segregated private schools. Black families were left to fend for themselves.

That lockout didn't last long. The closed schools were reopened in 1959 under court order. But in one Southside Virginia county the defiance continued unabated. Prince Edward County, where one of the *Brown* cases originated, managed to keep its public schools closed for a full five years, denying a generation of African-American children an education.

Among Virginia's major white-owned newspapers, only the *Virginian-Pilot*, my future employer, urged compliance with the *Brown* decision. Editor Lenoir Chambers' denouncement of Massive Resistance earned the paper its second Pulitzer Prize.[199]

By the time my family moved twenty miles east to Clarksville in 1965, Virginia school systems had established what was euphemistically called a "freedom of choice" policy that allowed black children to be admitted to white schools if their parents chose to send them. The result was token integration by a handful of brave African-American families.

There were only two black girls in my graduating class of one hundred at Bluestone High School. Looking back, I can only imagine that daily life for them was a living hell. When they were not being ostracized, they were being humiliated as the butt of racist jokes and pranks. I recall white boys on my school bus singing "Bye-Bye Blackbird" when the bus dropped off a black student at the end of the day. Even some teachers participated in the persecution. My senior English teacher—an otherwise capable and dedicated educator—mercilessly embarrassed the single black girl in the class in front of her peers when she couldn't come up with the answer to a question.

I didn't actively participate in the pervasive racist behavior, but I'm ashamed to say I didn't actively resist it either. Ultimately, it wasn't until after I graduated in 1967 that full integration was finally achieved by the wholesale reassignment of students. Bluestone became the senior high school and West End High

School, Uncle George's alma mater, became Bluestone Junior High School. Today Benjamin Sizemore, Uncle George's great-nephew, is the boys' basketball coach at my old school.

Integration was similarly slow to occur in Virginia's public colleges and universities, and when it did, it was only due to legal pressure from the federal government. In the fall of 1967, my freshman class of one thousand or so students at the College of William and Mary included the school's first residential African-American students: three young women who roomed together in a dormitory basement. They found themselves on a campus of strangers, encountering racist attitudes not just from students but from some professors as well, the women told a symposium at the college in 2016. "Our social life was with each other," said Lynn Briley, one of the three.[200]

When I joined the college marching band my freshman year, "Dixie" was still a standard part of the repertoire at football games. It was finally eliminated from our playlist in 1969, after the handful of black students on campus began protesting the song by burning a Confederate flag each time it was played.

My college years were a time of great social ferment. Like campuses across the country, William and Mary was roiled by student protests around a variety of issues, not the least of which was the Vietnam War. I was a committed opponent of the war, believing with the Reverend Martin Luther King Jr. that it was a tragic and immoral misuse of America's great power. In a famous speech in April 1967, King explained that he came to oppose the war as a natural outgrowth of his commitment to nonviolence in confronting the nation's racial woes. "I knew that I could never again raise my voice against the violence of the oppressed in the ghettoes," he said, "without having first spoken clearly to the greatest purveyor of violence in the world today: my own government."

The military draft was still in force when my college deferment ended with my graduation in 1971, so I applied to the

Mecklenburg County Draft Board for classification as a conscientious objector, seeking to be excused from military service. The three-man board initially turned me down, but I appealed and, on a two-to-one vote, the board reversed itself and granted my request. Between the two votes, the board got its first African-American member, who I firmly believe cast the deciding vote in my favor.

After college, I took over the editorship of the *Clarksville Times* upon my father's retirement. My wife joined the staff with me, and we took the newspaper's editorial stance in a dramatically different direction.

My father was not an overt racist. He was a gentle soul who never had an unkind word for anyone. But he was a man of his time and place. One of my keepsakes from that era is a pencil imprinted with this slogan: "*The Clarksville Times* proudly endorses segregation and states' rights."

My father's editorial policy reflected the views of the conservative establishment that held sway throughout Virginia and the South. In the 1964 presidential election he endorsed Arizona Senator Barry Goldwater, the right-wing nominee of the Republican Party, which was in the process of shedding its past as the party of emancipation in an effort to obtain Southern white votes. A principal pillar of Goldwater's campaign was his opposition to the landmark Civil Rights Act of 1964. And in 1968 my father endorsed third-party candidate George Wallace, the one-time Alabama governor who famously stood in the schoolhouse door to defy court-ordered integration and made a naked appeal for the votes of Southern racists.

By 1972 the realignment of the nation's political parties was complete. The Democrats threw off their history as the home of Southern segregationists, gave blacks and women unprecedented access to the party machinery, and nominated South Dakota Senator George McGovern for president on an antiwar platform. Under my editorship, the *Clarksville Times* endorsed McGovern.

As I look back on it, it occurs to me that longtime readers must have suffered a severe case of mental whiplash as they witnessed the transition.

Howard and Genevieve Sizemore, the author's parents, sit on the porch of the cabin Howard Sizemore preserved after his parents died. He had fond memories of spending time with the African-American blacksmith who lived there when he was a child. / John Sizemore

The *Times* not only endorsed McGovern, but also served as a home for the local insurgent Democrats, black and white, who volunteered for his campaign. We hosted several meetings of the biracial campaign committee in the *Times* building, where slave "hirelings" had toiled as tobacco-factory laborers a century before. At one point that fall, our advertising salesman came to me with a worried look on his face. There was talk around town, he said, that we were holding NAACP meetings in the building—an apparently unforgivable sin.

Readers might wonder how I escaped the pervasive prejudice of my small-town Southern childhood and emerged with an antiracist mindset. I don't have a pat answer to that question. One factor undoubtedly was the liberalizing influence of my college years. Many of my friends and classmates at William and Mary came from metropolitan areas and states outside the South where their minds had not been poisoned by bigotry. But I think I should also give some credit to my parents. My father's editorial stance notwithstanding, I never heard him or my mother express racist views around the house. They both grew up on farms before the rigid segregation of my youth had fully taken hold. The children of black sharecroppers were among their playmates. One of my father's most cherished childhood memories was of spending time with the old African-American blacksmith who lived in a log cabin on my grandfather's farm. After my grandparents died and their estate was split among their children, my father held onto the little patch of land where the cabin stood and kept it intact for many years.

If only by osmosis, I must have absorbed some lessons in tolerance.

Daffodil Graham visits Uncle George Sizemore at his home near Clarksville, VA.

* * * * *

As I glided through my segregated childhood in South Boston and Clarksville, Daffodil Graham was growing up twenty-five miles away in Roxboro, North Carolina—across both state and color lines. Neither of us was aware of the other's existence, or of the historical connection between our families: Daffodil's mother, Bertha, was a daughter of Jordan Sizemore, the second child of ex-slave Ben Sizemore's first marriage.

Daffodil's full name is Margaret Daffodil Graham. She long ago embraced her whimsical middle name, and that's how she is known by everyone in her family. Jovial and straight-talking, she hands out business cards featuring a drawing of a daffodil blossom.

I visited Daffodil on a crystal-clear spring day in 2013 at her home in Winston-Salem, North Carolina, where she retired after two careers as a teacher and social worker. Dressed in a navy blue running suit, a yellow T-shirt, and a colorful scarf that wrapped around her gray curls, she minced no words recalling her life in the waning days of Jim Crow.

Her father, whom she described as "the original deadbeat dad," was largely absent from her life. She was raised by her mother and a great-aunt. She went to school during the "separate but unequal" era, she told me. She could see the white high school from her back porch, but had to walk across town to all-black Person County High School. No bus was provided. When she passed the white elementary school, she would cross to the other side of the street, trying to get out of earshot of the racial epithets that were hurled at her from the playground.

One of Daffodil's most memorable walks home from school occurred during Hurricane Hazel, which brought a rare onslaught of drenching rains and howling winds to our inland region in 1954. I remember huddling with my mother and brother in the central hallway of our house until the storm blew over. Daffodil, meanwhile, made it home okay.

Daffodil Graham, 16, at her prom at all-black Person County High School in Roxboro, NC, in the 1960s.

Daffodil told me she has nothing but admiration for those African-American children who first broke the color barrier by attending white schools during the "freedom of choice" era—but she wouldn't have wanted to be one of them. "I praise God for them," she said. "But there's no way I would go through that. I'm not that good. I'm not a trailblazer. All that stress! A lot of high school is socialization. For those kids, their socialization was zero."[201]

Daffodil's mother worked in a chicken processing plant in Roxboro. After putting in a full shift, she would come home for a few hours of sleep and then go back at night to catch chickens in the brooder house where young chicks were raised. She also did housework and cooking for white families, setting aside part of her earnings in a college fund for Daffodil.

"She told me from the time I was a little girl, 'You will never walk in the back door of a white person's house,'" Daffodil said. "She was dead set that I would be a teacher. In that day, the highest pinnacle of success for an African-American was to teach."

Daffodil's mother acquired a set of encyclopedias, one volume at a time, as a premium for buying groceries at the local A&P, stimulating a lifelong love of books in her daughter.

Like everything else in Roxboro, the public libraries were segregated. "The black library was a tiny one-room log cabin on the other side of town with a few raggedy books," Daffodil told me. "But the white library was just down the street from our house. I would send my white friend Bill Short with his Radio Flyer wagon, and he'd fill it up with books. We'd split them up, and when we'd finished them, we'd trade off.

"You had to be inventive."

Jim Crow was ultimately dismantled piece by piece, propelled by the nonviolent activism espoused by Reverend King and other civil rights leaders. A sit-in by four black college students at a whites-only lunch counter in Greensboro, North Carolina, one hundred miles from Clarksville, in 1960 spurred similar protests around the country. Those actions—and the sometimes violent reaction by white authorities in the Deep South—paved the way for two key federal laws: the Civil Rights Act of 1964 banning racial discrimination in public accommodations and the Voting Rights Act of 1965 assuring African-Americans access to the ballot box.

After graduating from Fayetteville State University, Daffodil taught world history and geography at her alma mater, Person County High School, before going into social work. Divorced now, with a son and granddaughter, she is an active retiree who spends much of her time traveling. On a world map in her study, pushpins mark the forty-five US states and four continents she has visited. She traces her wanderlust back to those A&P encyclopedias.

"That's when I started reading about faraway places with strange-sounding names," she said.

* * * * *

The African-American Sizemore clan is full of teachers, reflecting that many share Daffodil's mother's profound faith in education as the path to a meaningful and satisfying life. That faith manifests in other ways as well. At the reunion each year, donations are solicited for the family scholarship fund for aspiring college students.

Three generations of Sizemores. From left: Evella Hutcheson, her mother Eugene Watkins, and her niece Krystle Watkins.

Another teacher in the family is Daffodil's cousin Evella Hutcheson. Her mother, Eugene Watkins, is a daughter of John Sizemore, the youngest child from Ben Sizemore's first marriage.

Evella's father, Ervin Watkins, was a sharecropper who died when Evella was twelve. The family lived on a series of farms in Mecklenburg County, including that of my uncle Roy Hobgood.

"I always said 'I'll never work on a farm,'" Evella told me. "My daddy never could get out of debt. He pushed me to be something better. I remember him urging me to do my math homework the night he died."[202]

After getting her bachelor's degree, Evella became a science teacher. She helped break the color barrier at Halifax County High School, a once all-white school I attended before moving to

Clarksville. In 1972 she was one of just seven African-Americans on a faculty of 135 teachers.

Miss Evella Watkins:
Consumer Math,
Human Biology

Evella Hutcheson, then Evella Watkins, was among a handful of black teachers at formerly all-white Halifax County High School in 1972. This photo is from Haliscope, the school yearbook. / Halifax County Public Library

"I always had to prove myself," she said. "Everything I did, I had to do it three times better than everybody else. I didn't think I was going to survive my first year there.

"Some white people aren't as smart as they think they are. Why have we been feeling we're inferior to them? I learned we're all the same."

Five years later, Evella was chairwoman of the science department. She won a full scholarship from the National Science Foundation and, while continuing to teach full time, commuted three days a week to Virginia State University in Petersburg, where she earned a master's degree in science education. "I told my students, 'You can do anything you set your mind to,'" she told me. Widowed and retired now after forty years of teaching, she still lives in Clarksville. Like Daffodil, she stayed in the South when many African-Americans were migrating north.

"My best friend in high school had her bags packed for New Jersey the day she graduated," Daffodil told me. "Kudos to those who stayed and tried to change things. All we were looking for was to be treated like human beings and to have the opportunity for a good job."

—9—

Howard

"What's in a name?" Juliet famously asks in *Romeo and Juliet*, Shakespeare's classic tale of starstruck lovers. It is Romeo's name, and nothing more, that makes him unacceptable to her kinfolk because the two lovers' families have been feuding for generations. So she urges Romeo to "doff thy name."

Though it is undeniably true that "a rose by any other name would smell as sweet," names still carry great weight. While some of us may not be overjoyed by the name our parents passed on to us, most of us consider it part and parcel of who we are and learn to live with it.

For a few, however, a name carries freight that is too much to bear. Such was the case for Howard el-Yasin.

In 1957 in New Haven, Connecticut, Howard was born Howard Walter Kent Sizemore. He was named for his father, Howard Sizemore, whose own father Bill arrived in New Haven in the 1930s and whose house became the gateway for other Mecklenburg County Sizemores joining the Great Migration.

In 2013 I spent a Saturday afternoon of bracing conversation with the younger Howard in his office in one of the Gothic stone buildings on the campus of Yale University, where he is assistant director of the Teaching Fellow Program in the Graduate School of Arts and Sciences. Soft-spoken, with short graying hair, he wore a faded blue T-shirt and wire-rim glasses.

As a teenager in the 1970s, Howard told me, he rejected the name Sizemore because it was the name of those who enslaved his ancestors. At the same time, he rejected Christianity, the religion his forebears absorbed from their masters, and embraced Islam. Yasin, the new name Howard chose for himself, is the name of the thirty-sixth chapter of the Qur'an.

Howard el-Yasin

"Muslims at that time presented themselves in opposition to all the things that represented the oppression of black people," he told me. "They were basically speaking against the notion that for black people, although we were slaves, Christianity was the only way toward redemption and the image of Christ as a white man on a cross was the only way to get to God, which just doesn't make any sense. Why would anyone believe that a human being alone could serve in that capacity? So that's the basic reason why I reject Christianity.

"And I'm not saying I reject people who are Christians, except those who are fanatics. I think what Islam teaches is that Christianity fits within the universe of God's love and worship of a higher being, but Islam absolutely rejects the notion of a human being being idolized in the name of God."[203]

He is less religious than he used to be, Howard said. He no longer considers himself an orthodox Muslim. He no longer prays five times a day, and he doesn't always participate in Islamic rituals like Ramadan.

"Ultimately, does it really matter if you say you're Buddhist or Muslim or Christian or Jewish? I don't think so," he said. "I consider myself a Muslim only because as human beings we feel it important to put names on things. But in the same breath that I say I consider myself a Muslim, I also say that I reject some aspects of what some Muslims call Islam. For instance, I'm gay. And I reject anything or any people or any culture or any ideology that rejects homosexuality as something that's wrong."

Islam has no monopoly on homophobia, Howard added. "I think you have to put things in the context of patriarchy. Religions are patriarchal. When it comes to sexuality, sexuality is controlled by men so that it becomes the function of procreation rather than pleasure. And the hypocrisy in most religions is that procreation is elevated and pleasure is devalued, except when it's done under the cloak or shadow of secrecy."

Over the years he has come to see that no religion, Islam included, has all the answers, Howard said. "There's fanaticism within every religion because religion itself is an opium set up to control societies. Why does everyone need to believe in the same God or believe that God is the same thing or God looks the same way? It's all about social order and control. I'm not passing any sort of moral judgment. I'm simply saying that's what it is."

I told Howard I got the distinct impression he is the rebel of the family. He laughed.

"Let's say I think outside the box," he said. "Sometimes people get nervous when I start talking. But I'm also very respectful. I don't have to believe or agree with what you're saying, but I'm respectful. That's the way I was raised."

* * * * *

When I met Howard, he and his life partner had been together for twenty-five years. He came out as gay to his father in the early days of the relationship, at a family reunion in Clarksville. His immediate family accepted him and his partner from day one, he said.

"I think deep down my family always knew I was gay, even when I was young. They may not have liked it, but I think they always knew."

I asked if most members of his extended family accept him for who and what he is.

"I can't say that I believe that," he said after a pause, adding, "I'm not going to name any names."

At this point in the interview, Howard asked me to turn off my tape recorder. Then he told me that, at the 2011 family reunion in Clarksville, he had proposed a change in the family bylaws to create a more welcoming atmosphere for households like his. As written, the bylaws said only blood relatives and spouses in Christian-sanctified marriages could hold leadership positions in the family. That meant someone like Howard's partner couldn't serve as an officer or as a host of the reunion.

Howard proposed a provision written in non-gender-specific language that would have opened up leadership positions to partners in common-law relationships. After heated discussion, the proposal was voted down.

"Some people said they thought it was un-Christian," Howard said.

Howard's partner was offended by the snub and said he didn't want to attend any more reunions. Howard was offended too. He said he couldn't make his kinfolk see that they were practicing a similar sort of discrimination to what they had experienced as African-Americans under Jim Crow.

"They don't see it as a double standard," he said. "They don't see that it's the same thing that's been done to them. To them, it's not Christian, and that's the end of it."

Howard didn't tell me this, but I learned independently that a leading voice in opposition to his proposal came from Charles Sizemore, the Christian preacher who discovered his mother thirty years after being orphaned. When I questioned him about the incident, Charles told me he advocated keeping the bylaws as they were because he believes homosexuality is wrong—a symptom of moral decay in society. He said he rejects any notion of equivalence between gay rights and racial equality.

Charles' position is consistent with a large body of opinion that still prevails in the Christian church and in African-American culture. Michael Eric Dyson, the noted African-American academic, author and Baptist preacher, has taken the black church to task for that attitude. "The black church, an institution that has been at the heart of black emancipation, refuses to unlock the oppressive closet for gays and lesbians," Dyson has written. "The deeply entrenched cultural and theological bias against gays and lesbians contradicts the love ethic at the heart of black Christianity. . . . Black Christians, who have been despised and oppressed for much of our existence, should be wary of extending that oppression to our lesbian sisters and black brothers."[204]

Charles was quick to assure me he was not judging Howard. Rather, his message to his cousin was "Let me just love *you*. Don't make me love what you *do*."

As for Howard, he felt that the opposition to his proposal was rooted in "outdated ideas." "Sometimes people want to bury things and think they'll go away. . . . I'm just as normal as anyone else. We shouldn't be denied because we haven't passed a sanctified litmus test."

Still, Howard was chastened by the experience. "I can't say that I'm just hankering to bring it up again," he said.

* * * * *

The fact that Howard went to some pains to try to change the status quo—and came to grief over it—suggested to me that his extended family is important to him, and I told him so.

"Absolutely," he replied. "Family means a lot. That's the way I was raised."

In many ways, he said, he is who he is today because of his grandparents, Bill and Ruby. Denied a decent life in the South, they came north to create better opportunities for themselves and their family, and he and his siblings are the beneficiaries of their sacrifices.

Howard attended historically black Morehouse College in Atlanta, but left after a year—for a variety of reasons, he said, including a general unease about being in the South. "I'm still a little uncomfortable about the South, especially the rural South," he admitted. "I view it as still perhaps more racist than I care to subject myself to. But I also think that Massachusetts is very racist. I've been called the N-word in Boston. All these things are relative. I've been called that in England too. I don't think there is a safe place for a person of color in the world."

He graduated from New England College in New Hampshire and worked for booksellers in Atlanta and New York before returning to New Haven to manage the museum store at the Yale art gallery. He also has a master's degree in liberal studies from Wesleyan University and, when I met him, was working on a master's of fine arts at Maryland Institute of Art. An artist specializing in sculpture and mixed media, he has a studio in West Haven, Connecticut. Some of his work was inspired by the lives of his grandparents.

"I don't know how true it is, but my grandfather told me about almost experiencing a lynching," he said. "He told me it was because he tried to kiss a white girl down in Virginia. That's always haunted me, that story. Some of my work is focused on lynching. I continue to explore that theme. . . .I think that older African-Americans in particular don't like to talk about it."

One of Howard's sculptures, titled *Blue Velvet Suitcase*, is a tribute to his grandmother, who worked as a housekeeper her whole adult life—including at Yale, where she retired. The centerpiece of the sculpture is the 1930s suitcase she brought with her when she migrated north. Howard took out its insides and lined it with blue velvet.

"The piece is really about a lack of comfort," he said. "This institution—an elitist institution which is supposed to provide comfort—didn't provide her any. It really denied her comfort, because all she did was clean toilets.

"I think that there have always been good white people and good black people and bad white people and bad black people. . . . It's always a struggle. It's like those people who say that we're all God's children, but they want to exclude some people from the table because they're gay. That you can quote me on. I think that race and sexuality or any other type of oppression or discrimination are all in the same basket. It doesn't matter.

"And I'm not saying that the brutal, physical oppression of black people should be diminished by equating the oppression of people based on their sexuality and race. What I'm saying is that any oppression is wrong.

"I'm saying an injustice to one is injustice to all."

* * * * *

During my conversation with Howard—which occurred in the fifth year of the Barack Obama administration—I asked Howard to what extent he believes things have gotten better for African-Americans.

"Well, we have a black president," he said. "But then, all of the haters have come out of the closet. So have they really gotten better? They've gotten better in that legally it can happen. But then all of the naysayers, the fanatics, have just become fanatical. It is the world we live in."

Then in 2016, Donald Trump was elected president. The reality-show host had built his national following in large part by peddling the racist lie that Obama was born outside the United States and therefore was an illegitimate president. Once elected, he wasted no time proclaiming an agenda calculated to dismantle Obama's legacy.

When I caught up with Howard after Trump took office, he had nothing good to say about the new regime in Washington. "In one word, I would say it's disgusting," he said.

"He has some personal psychological issues," Howard said. "He incites racism. . . . I think we need a new movement, a movement of the people—and by the people I mean those who care about an open society, a more egalitarian and humane society, a more democratic society."

He is already nostalgic for Obama, Howard added. "I am extremely proud that he supported LGBT rights. . . . He was the first intersectional president. He understands what it is to be queer, to be a woman, to be different, living in the most diverse country and culture on the face of the earth, and recognizing the equity that every human being deserves."

Michael Eric Dyson put it this way: "We have, in the span of a few years, elected the nation's first black president and placed in the Oval Office the scariest racial demagogue in a generation. The two may not be unrelated."[205]

A few days after Trump's inauguration, I had lunch with Uncle George and his great-niece Evella Hutcheson. Like Howard and African-Americans everywhere, they took immense pride in Obama's accomplishments and were disconsolate about our new president's determination to undo them. Both of them had been following the news closely. Uncle George said he frequently sits up until 4:00 a.m. watching an obscure all-news TV channel. He and Evella have become increasingly alarmed about where Trump plans to take the country. Uncle George said he is worried by Trump's autocratic tendencies and fears he will get the country into a war, perhaps even deploy the nation's nuclear arsenal. "It's scary," Uncle George said. "This is a democracy, not a dictatorship."

Trump was put in office by millions of angry white men who felt their privileged status threatened by the rise of women and minorities, Evella said. And while African-Americans voted against him in overwhelming numbers, they failed to turn out at the same levels they did for Obama.

"I've never seen a president like this in my life," Evella said. "He has no moral values. I think he's got a mental problem."

"It's a sad situation," Uncle George agreed. But then, summoning up his customary optimism, he added, "We'll get through it."

Yes, Evella said, "God will take care of us."

—10—

Truth and Reconciliation

The story of the black and white Sizemores of Mecklenburg County is the story of American apartheid in microcosm.

In 1900, my great-grandmother Mary Catherine Gold Sizemore lived on a farm on the south side of the Dan River, just downstream from my slave-owning ancestor's homestead, with five of her six surviving children. She was recently widowed: my great-grandfather Thomas Ledford Sizemore, the Civil War soldier who was wounded at Gettysburg, had died of cancer in 1898 at age fifty-eight. Richard—the couple's eldest son, my grandfather—was the only one who lived elsewhere. In 1899, he had married my grandmother, Georgia Snead Sizemore, in a country church just over the Halifax County line ten miles away. After the ceremony, the newlyweds traveled by horse and buggy to Mary Catherine's place for something called an "infair"—a bountiful turkey dinner at the groom's family home, a tradition in that time and place.

That much I knew from my family's oral history. What I didn't know, until I began scouring census records while researching this book, was that Mary Catherine's home was surrounded by African-American Sizemore households.

Next door lived Daniel Sizemore, Uncle George's grandfather, born into slavery in 1834, with his wife of twenty-eight years, the former Mariah Overbey, and their son Nathaniel.[206] Daniel and a half dozen other Sizemore freedmen had been living a stone's throw from my ancestors for more than three decades, almost certainly as sharecroppers.

That 1900 listing is Daniel's last appearance in the census records. I presume he died between 1900 and 1910, although I have been unable to locate a death record. No one knows where he is buried.

Richard Sizemore and his bride Georgia Snead, the author's grandparents, on their wedding day, December 10, 1899.

Meanwhile, his descendants began joining the Great Migration, fleeing the Jim Crow strictures, political disenfranchisement, lack of economic opportunity, and racist violence that had taken hold across the South. That American apartheid was so rigid, so complete, that within a few more decades the ties that had bound the black and white Sizemores together had been erased from both families' collective memory. A century later, when I encountered Uncle George and his kinfolk, we met as total strangers, each of us unaware of our shared history. Our families, who once lived side by side, had been torn asunder by an invisible wall. We lived in separate neighborhoods, went to separate schools, attended separate churches. That wall, like white Southerners' animosity toward our black neighbors, has begun to break down over the past half-century, but we've got a long way to go.

I don't mean to romanticize the relationship that connected our ancestors. It was, of course, grossly unequal, both before and after emancipation. I only mean to say that I think we need to acknowledge and confront it, in all its ugliness.

For a century and a half now, a lot of Southerners have done their best to whitewash the nation's history of racial inequity—to rewrite it, bury it, blot it out. I once heard a historian call it "self-induced amnesia." I believe we need to lance the great national wound of slavery before we can heal from it.

That same historian had a term for this process. He called it "cleansing ourselves with the detergent of truth."[207] Perhaps we need something like what occurred in South Africa after the end of that country's apartheid system: a Truth and Reconciliation Commission to expose and acknowledge the injustices of the past and work toward forgiveness and healing.

To anyone who doubts our nation is in need of healing, I can only say this: Open your eyes. Look around you. The legal underpinnings of Jim Crow have been dismantled, but its legacy remains. In many places our schools, neighborhoods, and churches are as segregated as ever. By virtually any measurable social indicator, there is a vast chasm between the life prospects of black and white Americans.

In 2013, the median white household's net worth was *thirteen times* that of black households.[208] In black America, poverty rates are 145 percent higher,[209] infant mortality is 130 percent higher,[210] and unemployment is double that of whites.[211] Young black males are twenty-one times more likely than whites to be shot dead by police.[212] One-third of black males born today can expect to go to prison sometime in their lifetimes.[213] Blacks and whites use illegal drugs at roughly the same rates, but blacks are incarcerated at six times the rate of whites for drug offenses.[214]

As a white male born into a middle-class household, I was afforded benefits and opportunities according to my skin color and history—a history that almost no blacks would have been able to call theirs. I grew up in a stable family in a comfortable home and never lacked for life's necessities. I suffered none of the indignities of Jim Crow. My extended family was part of the local power structure: One of my cousins was mayor of Clarksville in the 1960s. An uncle was mayor of South Boston in the 1950s, and two more of my uncles served in succession as clerk of the circuit court in Halifax County. The position made them key cogs in the segregationist political machine run by Harry Byrd, one-time governor and later US senator, that controlled Virginia politics for half a century.

As a result of my family's relative affluence and connections, my parents were able to pay for me to attend one of the best colleges in the country, where I got preferential treatment in the admissions process because my father and several uncles and cousins preceded me there. When I declared my conscientious objection to military service during the Vietnam War, I paid no personal price for it—unlike the great African-American boxer Muhammad Ali, whose antiwar stance cost him his heavyweight title. And thanks to a family connection (my father), I was able to walk into a job as a weekly newspaper editor at age twenty-three, which prepared me for a forty-five-year career in journalism without a single day of unemployment.

As a beneficiary of white privilege, I have only just come to realize that I stand on the backs of the millions of Africans and their progeny who played an integral part in building this nation with no compensation for their labors, often under the most inhumane conditions.

And my story is just one of many. My ancestor was one of more than fifty thousand slave owners in Virginia and nearly four hundred thousand across the South in 1860. Moreover, many if not most other Southern whites benefited from the economic system those slaves propped up—to say nothing of the slave traders, bankers, and other businessmen in the North who made fortunes off it.

Belated as it was, learning my family's history compelled me to do something positive with the knowledge. For starters, I decided to scale that invisible wall and reach out to the descendants of those my ancestors enslaved. From the moment I met them, they have been unfailingly warm, kind and generous with their time and good humor. We have become good friends.

Charles Sizemore, the onetime orphan and retired preacher, once told me he had a dream that one day our simultaneous family reunions would become one consolidated, multihued gathering. We haven't reached that point, but we have made a start.

As far as I know, my efforts have stirred no ill will among my relatives. Several of them, especially among the younger generation, have expressed interest in sharing my explorations.

But the decades-long reunion traditions on both sides of the color divide are not easily upended. My family's annual potluck supper traditionally occurs at the exact same time as the African-American Sizemores' big banquet, and we are all creatures of habit. Neither family seems inclined to give up its own annual tradition in favor of a combined gathering.

Nevertheless, in 2013, with the two reunions going on ten miles apart, I invited the black Sizemores to stop by our gathering for a get-acquainted visit in the afternoon before the evening events. To my delight, a convoy of about a dozen—led by Uncle George—showed up. About the same number of my relatives had arrived at the church social hall where we always meet, within sight of the cemetery where my grandparents and other forebears are buried. The two families mingled pleasantly for an hour or so. I have the pictures to prove it!

As our visitors drove off late that afternoon, my cousin Dan leaned over to me and said, "That sound you hear is my father rolling over in his grave."

In 2015, when the black Sizemore reunion returned to Mecklenburg County, I asked Evella Hutcheson, one of the hosts, to put me on the program for the banquet. I gave the family a progress report on my research and said I hoped that telling our story would contribute in some small way toward healing the country's racial wounds.

During their simultaneous family reunions in 2013, the black and white Sizemore families had a get-acquainted visit. The author is on the far left, in the tie-dyed shirt.

"White Americans have a lot to atone for, and we need to say it plainly," I told them. "My family stole your family's liberty, their labor, and their human dignity. And I'm sorry."

The family responded with their customary warmth, enveloping me with hugs and kind words.

* * * * *

I recently came to know a kindred spirit across the country named Tom DeWolf. Like me, Tom discovered late in life that there were racial skeletons in his family's closet. But there is a key difference between us: he is not a Southerner.

Tom grew up in a mostly white environment in southern California and now lives in Oregon. In his late forties, he discovered to his shock that he is descended from the most successful slave-trading family in American history, the DeWolfs of Rhode Island, who were responsible for transporting at least ten thousand Africans to the Americas.

Tom and nine other family members embarked on a memorable journey in which they retraced their ancestors' steps from New England to West Africa to the Caribbean, uncovering a long-buried history. He wrote a book about it—*Inheriting the Trade,* published in 2008—which lays bare the extent to which slavery was an all-American phenomenon, not just a Southern one. In fact, the majority of slave trading in America was done by Northerners. The DeWolf family's journey of discovery was also the subject of a documentary film, *Traces of the Trade,* produced by one of Tom's cousins.

In 2012 Tom published a second book, *Gather at the Table,* with coauthor Sharon Morgan, an African-American woman from Chicago whose ancestors were enslaved in the Deep South. The book is an account of their joint odyssey to explore their roots and to grapple with slavery's lingering legacy.

Now, Tom is executive director of Coming to the Table, a nonprofit organization based at Eastern Mennonite University in Harrisonburg, Virginia, which seeks to promote racial healing, in large part by bringing together descendants of enslavers and the enslaved. It was founded by descendants of Thomas Jefferson, who is now widely acknowledged to have fathered several children with his slave Sally Hemings, and of the Hairstons, a family that owned thousands of slaves on dozens of plantations stretching from Virginia to Mississippi. The group draws its inspiration from the Rev. Martin Luther King Jr.'s vision, laid out in his 1963 "I Have a Dream" speech, that one day "the sons of former slaves and the sons of former slave owners will be able to sit down together at the table of brotherhood."

It was Tom DeWolf who opened my eyes to the physical extent of slavery's scars on African-Americans. He told me that a relatively young field of science called epigenetics is helping to explain how the historical trauma of slavery is passed down to its modern descendants. Recent studies suggest that traumatic experiences can produce molecular scars adhering to a person's

DNA that are then passed along to his or her children and grandchildren.

"We inherit in multiple ways the history of the past," Tom told me. "We created a system in this nation of white supremacy that benefits somebody like me and harms people like my coauthor Sharon, and that gets passed down. . . . It's in our DNA. So it's physical as well as social."[215]

After Barack Obama was elected president in 2008, the veteran African-American columnist Clarence Page wrote that a key to Obama's success was his lack of any ancestry rooted in American slavery. "Being raised by his white mother and grandparents in multiracial Hawaii and Indonesia," Page wrote, "he was spared the post-traumatic slavery syndrome that for many of us African-Americans has been a cultural crippler."[216]

Some white Americans commonly retort that they can't be held responsible for the actions of their slave-owning ancestors, and that the plight of slavery's present-day descendants isn't their problem. I asked Tom DeWolf how he would respond to that mindset.

"If in fact we want to live up to the ideals upon which this nation was founded, then I *am* responsible," he said. "I don't feel any particular guilt about what my ancestors did, but I do feel a responsibility to fix the inequities that exist. And part of that is acknowledging that we don't have a level playing field. We live in a system that continues to benefit people that look like me. And it's not just a black and white issue. I benefit from being male instead of female, from being raised Christian instead of Muslim, straight instead of gay, able-bodied instead of having a disability, being middle-class instead of poor. In every aspect of who I am, I carry privilege."

Tom confesses in his most recent book that his exploration of slavery's legacy has left him more pessimistic about healing America's racial divide than when he began his journey. Getting to know his coauthor made him see what a deep psychic wound she carries around with her every day, he told me. "Knowing all of that, you understand the wound better and you realize just how serious and pervasive it is," he said. "It makes me not very optimistic about our chances. And yet I'm still responsible for doing what I can."

The first step is talking about it. And that is a difficult step to take—on both sides of the color line.

"It's not just white folks that don't talk about this," Tom said. "I think a lot of white folks avoid it for many reasons, among them guilt and shame. But there's a lot of black folks who also don't have this conversation. In the book Sharon talks about how in her family, people didn't want to talk about it. People didn't want to deal with the horror of the past."

I have been told the same thing by members of the African-American Sizemore family. And in one instance, I got a stark reminder of how off-limits the topic can be.

In the latter stages of my research, I learned of an African-American Sizemore with no known connection to Uncle George's family. Thinking and hoping this person might be a descendant of one of the other Sizemore slaves, I reached out by e-mail, asking if the person might consent to an interview. I was unprepared for the response I got.

The person works at a university. A few days later I received an e-mail from an investigator at the campus police department telling me in no uncertain terms that the person wanted no further contact with me. If I made any further attempts, I was told, a "police report for harassment will be made and criminal charges may be brought against you."[217]

Needless to say, I desisted.

Yet if there is any hope of resolving what may well be the preeminent issue tearing our nation apart today, we need to talk about it. And it must be a deep discussion, not a superficial one. To make this point, Tom DeWolf offered a medical analogy.

"If you've got skin cancer, you're not going to try and cure it with Clearasil," he said. "You're actually going to try and understand what it is that you have and what led to it, what's the history of it, so that you can avoid it in the future, and then what's the treatment protocol with the best chances of curing it."

I attended Coming to the Table's National Gathering in Harrisonburg in June 2016, joining a multihued group of about one hundred people dedicated to bridging our nation's racial divide. Some, like me, were the descendants of enslavers. Some were the descendants of slaves. And some had ancestors on both sides of the peculiar institution.

It was an emotional weekend marked by frequent expressions of shame, guilt, angst, and anger, punctuated occasionally by tears. Several participants said members of their own families remain in denial about their ancestors' role in slavery. One woman choked up when she told of family members who stopped speaking to her after she published the story of the family's slave-owning past on a genealogy website.

The last night of the gathering featured group singing, poetry reading, and a broom-jumping ceremony, a recreation of an old slave marriage ritual. The next morning, before leaving for home, we all joined hands in a circle around a maple tree on a grassy hillside, accompanied by the beat of bongo drums and the smell of burning sage. Butterflies floated by on a gentle breeze and birdsong rose to the sky under a brilliant sun. A chalice of water was passed around the circle and participants were invited to call out to their ancestors for strength and wisdom.

On a moonless night a few months later, I joined a smaller group from Coming to the Table's Richmond chapter for an immersive guided hike along Richmond's Slave Trail Walk, a serpentine path along a bluff on the south shore of the James River. One of our guides told us slaves were typically brought into and out of the city at night to avoid offending the tender sensibilities of Richmond's society matrons.

The trail begins near the docks where slaves were shipped in and out of Virginia's capital city and ends in Shockoe Bottom, where slaves were bought and sold in the shadow of the state capitol designed by Thomas Jefferson. We walked single file, tethered together by a rope around our waists in the style of a slave coffle, holding torches aloft against the cool breeze that blew off the river. Another of our guides portrayed a slave driver, berating us in demeaning terms, forbidding us to speak, and ordering us to walk faster.

At the end of our walk, we talked about the experience. I felt emotionally wrung out—and I wasn't the only one. "I felt totally alone, disempowered and full of rage," one man said. "I knew it was make-believe, but it was still traumatizing," said another.

* * * * *

I first heard of Coming to the Table at a conference on the legacy of slavery at Randolph College in Lynchburg, Virginia, in 2014. One of the speakers was Art Carter, a retired physician who is active in a local affiliate of the organization on the Eastern Shore of Virginia. As a descendant of European-Americans, African-Americans, and Native Americans, Art brought an all-inclusive perspective to the discussion. Some of his family identify as European-American, some as African-American, some as Native American, and some as various combinations of ethnicities, Art told me in a later interview. But all are made welcome at their annual family reunions, which began in 2007.

"We all acknowledge and love each other," he said. "We're a rainbow."

I asked Art how optimistic he is that America will ever fully heal its racial wounds. He said it's necessary to take a long view.

"We go forward and then backward, but like Dr. King, I think the arc seems to be progressing forward," he said. "As long as there are people who believe we are all brothers and sisters, I'm very much optimistic. I think we'll eventually get there."[218]

He spoke of the "bittersweet link" between descendants of enslavers and the enslaved. "BitterSweet: Linked Through Slavery" is the name of a blog established by Coming to the Table that allows those linked descendants to explore their shared ties to slavery and its legacy in search of reconciliation.

That struck a chord with me. The relationship between descendants of enslavers and the enslaved is bitter because of the horrible inequity and inhumanity of slavery, yet also sweet because of the genuine bonds of affection that once existed, at least in some cases and on some level, between our ancestors before being severed during the apartheid era. I believe—no, I know, based on the warmth and conviviality I have found in the company of the African-American Sizemores—that those bonds can be restored, this time on a level playing field.

What it takes, as Dr. King told us half a century ago, is for us to come together at the table of brotherhood.

An African-American friend of mine once told me it's naïve to think that telling the Sizemores' story can help undo four centuries of American racism. And she is no doubt right. I plead guilty to naïveté. But I am still determined to do what I can.

"We got into this mess together," Art Carter said, "and we've got to get out of it together."[219]

We can, and we must.

Acknowledgements

From the get-go, this book has been a labor of love. It would not have been possible without a robust support network. Many thanks are due my wife Mary Kay for her emotional support, inspiration, and technical assistance; my daughter Julie for her excellent design work on the book cover; my other daughter Jennie for building my website; my friend and colleague Denise Bridges for her thoughtful suggestions on improving the manuscript; my publisher Robert Pruett, who took a chance on a late-blooming novice author; and my editor Erin Harpst for her perceptive and meticulous work guiding the book into print. I am also eternally grateful to all the African-American Sizemores who opened their hearts and homes and shared their stories with me. Particular thanks are due Evella Hutcheson, my "fixer" who smoothed the way for me with the family, assuring them I was worthy of their trust. I hope I have earned it. Most of all I am grateful to Uncle George for his wisdom, friendship and good humor. He is one of a kind, and I am a better person for having known him.

Bill Sizemore

About the Author

Bill Sizemore
/Stephen Katz, The Virginian-Pilot

Bill Sizemore grew up in segregated small-town Virginia and spent forty-three years as a journalist, most of that time at the *Virginian-Pilot*, the state's largest newspaper, where he was a Pulitzer Prize finalist in 2007. He wrote about topics as varied as state government and politics, televangelist Pat Robertson, the private military company Blackwater, and Virginia's prison-building boom. He has also written for the Associated Press, *Ms.* magazine and *Virginia Quarterly Review*. Since his retirement in 2014, he has focused on his two highest priorities: playing with his grandchildren and writing books. He lives in Williamsburg, Virginia.

Also by Bill Sizemore:

A Far, Far Better Thing: Did a Fatal Attraction Lead to a Wrongful Conviction? co-written with Jens Soering, Lantern Books, 2017

billsizemorebooks.com

Profits from sales of Uncle George and Me *are donated to the Benjamin Sizemore Educational Scholarship and Recognition Fund.*

Endnotes

Introduction

1. Christy Coleman, remarks given at "Facing the Past, Freeing the Future: Slavery's Legacy, Freedom's Promise," a symposium at Randolph College, Lynchburg, VA, April 2014.

Chapter 1

2. H.F. Hutcheson, "A Brief History of Mecklenburg County," published in the *South Hill Enterprise*, South Hill, VA, March 3, 1922.

3. John W. Tisdale, *The Story of the Occoneechees* (Richmond, VA: Dietz Press, 1953), 23.

4. Ibid., 45.

5. Raymond J. DeMallie, "Tutelo and Neighboring Groups." In *Southeast*, edited by Raymond D. Fogelson. Handbook of North American Indians, edited by William C. Sturtevant, vol. 14 (Washington, DC: Smithsonian Institution Press, 2004), 291.

6. James D. Rice, *Tales from a Revolution: Bacon's Rebellion and the Transformation of Early America* (New York: Oxford University Press, 2012), 27.

7. Ethan A. Schmidt, *The Divided Dominion: Social Conflict and Indian Hatred in Early Virginia* (Boulder: University Press of Colorado, 2015), 164.

8. Rice, 45.

9. Jeffrey and Kathryn St. John, *Landmarks, 1765–1990: A Brief History of Mecklenburg County, Virginia* (Boydton, VA: Mecklenburg County Board of Supervisors, 1990), 15.

10. Schmidt, 171.

11. Thomas L. Long, Martin H. Quitt, and the *Dictionary of American Biography*, "Byrd, William (1674-1744)," in *Encyclopedia Virginia*, Virginia Foundation for the Humanities. Article published April 13, 2009, last modified January 6, 2016, http://www.EncyclopediaVirginia.org/Byrd_William_1674-1744.

12. William Byrd II, *A Journey to the Land of Eden: In the Year 1733, in The Westover Manuscripts*, electronic transcription of the first edition (Petersburg: Edmund and Julian C. Ruffin, 1841; Chapel Hill: University of North Carolina, 2001), 105, http://docsouth.unc.edu/nc/byrd/byrd.html.

13. Emory G. Evans and the *Dictionary of Virginia Biography*, "William Byrd III," History.org, accessed November 10, 2017, http://www.history.org/almanack/people/bios/biowbyrd.cfm.

14. Deed dated October 30, 1765, Skipwith Family Papers, Special Collections Research Center, Swem Library, College of William and Mary.

15. Tisdale, 80.

16. Rice, 191.

17. Brendan Wolf, "Racial Integrity Laws (1924-1930)," in *Encyclopedia Virginia*, Virginia Foundation for the Humanities. Article published February 17, 2009, last modified November 4, 2015, https://www.encyclopediavirginia.org/Racial_Integrity_Laws_of_the_1920s.

18. John "Blackfeather" Jeffries, interview by the author, July 2015.

19. Pete Seeger, vocal performance of "All Mixed Up," arr. Louis Bennett-Coverley, conducted by Paul Halley, recorded at Living Music Studio, Litchfield, CT, with Gaudeamus (chorus, arr.

Paul Halley), Paul Prestopino (mandolin), Joanie Madden (pennywhistle), Gordon Gottlieb (percussion), on *Pete*, Living Music Studio LMUS-0032, released April 16, 1996, compact disc. Originally released in 1965.

20. Nell Irvin Painter, *The History of White People* (New York: W.W. Norton, 2010), 391.

21. James Baldwin. "On Being 'White'. . . and Other Lies," *Essence*, April 1984, 92.

22. Theodore W. Allen, *The Origin of Racial Oppression in Anglo-America*, The Invention of the White Race, vol. 2 (London: Verso Books, 2012), x.

23. Rice, 101.

24. Edmund S. Morgan, *American Slavery, American Freedom: The Ordeal of Colonial Virginia* (New York: W.W. Norton, 1975), 328.

Chapter 2

25. Michael Eric Dyson, *The Michael Eric Dyson Reader* (New York: Basic Civitas Books, 2004), 83.

26. Mecklenburg County Land Records, Virginia, Deed Book 3, p. 483, Mecklenburg County Courthouse, Boydton, VA.

27. Ibid., multiple entries.

28. 1840 US Census, Mecklenburg County, VA, population schedule, West District, p. 21, https://www.ancestrylibrary.com, and 1860 US Census, 22nd Regiment Mecklenburg County, slave schedule, p. 21, https://www.ancestrylibrary.com.

29. Joseph C. Robert, *The Road from Monticello: A Study of the Virginia Slavery Debate of 1832* (New York: AMS Press, 1941), 115.

30. Schmidt, 68.

31. Susan Dunn, *Dominion of Memories: Jefferson, Madison & the Decline of Virginia* (New York: Basic Books, 2007), 48.

32. Robert, 67.

33. Ibid., 83.

34. Ibid.

35. Thomas Jefferson to John Holmes, 22 April 1820, in the Paul Mellon Bequest, Accession #11619, Special Collections, University of Virginia Library.

36. Robert, 89.

37. Ibid., 35.

38. Ibid., 43.

39. Ibid., 46.

40. "Measuring Race," American Anthropological Association. Article last modified April 7, 2016, accessed November 10, 2017, http://www.understandingrace.org/history/science/measuring_race.html.

41. Ervin L. Jordan Jr., *Black Confederates and Afro-Yankees in Civil War Virginia* (Charlottesville: University Press of Virginia, 1995), 160.

42. Charles L. Perdue Jr., Thomas E. Barden, and Robert K. Phillips, eds., *Weevils in the Wheat: Interviews with Virginia Ex-Slaves* (Charlottesville: University Press of Virginia, 1976), 92.

43. Perdue et al., 34.

44. Jordan, 162.

45. Perdue et al., 290.

46. James H. Cone, *The Spirituals and the Blues: An Interpretation* (New York: Seabury Press, 1972), 23.

47. Samuel Chi-Yuen Lowe, "The Challenge of Freedom: Baptists, Slavery and Virginia, 1760–1810" (PhD diss., University of California, Berkeley, 2003), 225.

48. Perdue et al., 84.

49. Harriet A. Jacobs, *Incidents in the Life of a Slave Girl* (New York: Oxford University Press, 1987), 27.

50. Ibid., 49.

51. Ibid., 47.

52. Painter, 122.

53. Cone, 22.

54. Annette Gordon-Reed, *The Hemingses of Monticello: An American Family* (New York: W.W. Norton, 2008), 48.

55. Avory Estate v. Administrator of Avory Estate, Mecklenburg County (VA) Chancery Causes, 1854, 1854-009, Local Government Records Collection, Mecklenburg County court records, Library of Virginia, Richmond.

56. 1870 US Census, Mecklenburg County, VA, population schedule, Clarksville Township, p. 81, https://www.ancestrylibrary.com.

57. MacKasey & Wife's Estate v. Executor of Roberts Estate, Mecklenburg County (VA) Chancery Causes, 1854, 1854-016, Local Government Records Collection, Mecklenburg County court records, Library of Virginia, Richmond.

58. Birth register, Mecklenburg County, VA, 1853, p. 13, microfilm, reel 25, Library of Virginia, Richmond.

59. Birth register, Mecklenburg County, VA, 1860, p. 96, ibid.

60. Brenda E. Stevenson, *Life in Black & White: Family and Community in the Slave South* (New York: Oxford University Press, 1996), 182.

Chapter 3

61. *Mecklenburg County, Virginia: Largest Slaveholders from 1860 Slave Census Schedules,* transcribed by Tom Blake, August 2003, accessed November 13, 2017, http://freepages.genealogy.rootsweb.ancestry.com/~ajac/vamecklenburg.htm (site offline for updates as of this printing).

62. John Owen Allen, "Tobacco, Slaves and Secession: Southside Virginia on the Brink of the Great Rebellion" (PhD diss., Catholic University of America, 2003), 121.

63. Birth register, Mecklenburg County, VA, 1859, p.78, microfilm, reel 25, Library of Virginia, Richmond.

64. *Mecklenburg County, Virginia: Largest Slaveholders.*

65. *Tobacco Plant* (Clarksville, VA), September 8, 1858.

66. "Tragical Occurrence—A Negro Killed," *Tobacco Plant*, October 14, 1859.

67. *Tobacco Plant*, November 25, 1859.

68. Editorial, ibid., December 10, 1859.

69. *Tobacco Plant*, November 16, 1860.

70. Editorial, ibid., November 23, 1860.

71. *Tobacco Plant*, December 7, 1860.

72. Alexander H. Stephens, "Cornerstone Speech" (Savannah, GA, March 21, 1861), transcribed by the *Savannah Republican*, reprinted in Henry Cleveland, *Alexander H. Stephens, in Public and Private: With Letters and Speeches, before, during, and since the War* (Philadelphia: National Publishing Company, 1866), 717–729, https://www.ucs.louisiana.edu/~ras2777/amgov/stephens.html.

73. Susan Bracey, *Life by the Roaring Roanoke* (Mecklenburg County, VA: Mecklenburg County Bicentennial Commission, 1977), 301.

74. *Tobacco Plant*, April 5, 1861.

75. Ibid., May 10, 1861.

76. Edward R. Crews and Timothy A. Parrish, *14ᵗʰ Virginia Infantry*, The Virginia Regimental Histories Series, (Lynchburg, VA: H.E. Howard, 1995), 140.

77. Eric Foner, *Reconstruction: America's Unfinished Revolution, 1863–1877* (New York: Harper & Row, 1988), 15.

78. Crews and Parrish, 140.

79. Ibid.

80. Ibid.

81. Ibid., 42.

82. Gen. J.D. Imboden, "Lee at Gettysburg," *Mecklenburg Herald* (Boydton, VA), April 26, 1871.

83. Crews and Parrish, 140.

84. Patti O. Weaver and Jeffrey C. Weaver, *Reserves*, The Virginia Regimental Histories Series, (Appomattox, VA: H.E. Howard, 2002), 83.

85. Requisitions of Slaves and Free Negroes, Mecklenburg County, n.d., Free Negro and Slave Records, 1781–1882. Local Government Records Collection, Mecklenburg County court records, Library of Virginia, Richmond.

86. James H. Brewer, *The Confederate Negro: Virginia's Craftsmen and Military Laborers, 1861–1865* (Durham, NC: Duke University Press, 1969), 150.

87. Requisitions of Slaves and Free Negroes, ibid.

88. Leon F. Litwack, *Been in the Storm So Long: The Aftermath of Slavery* (New York: Alfred A. Knopf: distributed by Random House, 1979), 38.

89. Jordan, 260.

90. Bracey, 280.

91. Mecklenburg County Court Order Book No. 7, May 1861, p. 295, Library of Virginia, Richmond.

92. Litwack, *Been in the Storm*, 30.

93. Ibid., 43.

94. Ibid., 75.

95. Kevin M. Levin, *Remembering the Battle of the Crater: War as Murder* (Lexington: University Press of Kentucky, 2012), 27.

96. Litwack, *Been in the Storm*, 91.

97. Levin, 31.

98. Crews and Parrish, 140.

99. Litwack, *Been in the Storm*, 169.

100. W.E.B. DuBois, *Black Reconstruction* (New York: Harcourt Brace, 1935), 111.

101. Crews and Parrish, 140.

102. Guy Gugliotta, "New Estimate Raises Civil War Death Toll," *New York Times*, April 2, 2012, http://www.nytimes.com/2012/04/03/science/civil-war-toll-up-by-20-percent-in-new-estimate.html.

103. Nelson Morehouse Blake, *William Mahone of Virginia: Soldier and Political Insurgent* (Richmond, VA: Garret & Massie, 1935), 72.

104. DuBois, 124.

Chapter 4

105. George Sizemore, interview by the author, September 2010.

106. 1870 US Census, Mecklenburg County, VA, population schedule, Clarksville Township, p. 5, https://www.ancestrylibrary.com.

107. George Sizemore, interview by the author, August 2011.

108. Bracey, 293.

109. Mecklenburg County Court Order Book No. 7, July 1864, p. 561, Library of Virginia, Richmond.

110. Philip J. Schwarz, *Twice Condemned: Slaves and the Criminal Laws of Virginia, 1705–1865* (Baton Rouge: Louisiana State University Press, 1988), ix.

111. Mecklenburg County Court Order Book No. 7, July 1864, p. 562, Library of Virginia. Richmond.

112. John Guilfoyle to Office of the Provost Marshal, 14 December 1865, *Records of the Field Office for the State of Virginia, Bureau of Refugees, Freedmen, and Abandoned Lands 1865–1872*, microfilm M1913, (Washington, DC: National Archives and Records Administration, 2006) (hereafter cited as *Field Office Records 1865–1872*).

113. Cohabitation register, *Field Office Records 1865–1872*, ibid.

114. Labor contract dated 5 January 1866, *Field Office Records 1865–1872*, ibid.

115. DuBois, 130.

116. George W. Graham to Gen. Orlando Brown, assistant commissioner, 28 January 1868, *Field Office Records 1865–1872*, vol. 142, April 1867–December 1868, roll 59.

117. Graham to Brown, 30 May, 1868, ibid.

118. Register of Complaints, Case No. 7, 20 February 1867, *Field Office Records 1865–1872*, vol. 143, January 1867–November 1868, p. 4, roll 60.

119. Litwack, *Been in the Storm*, 474.

120. Ibid., 472.

121. Graham to Brown, 28 January 1868, *Field Office Records 1865–1872*, vol. 142, April 1867–December 1868, roll 59.

122. Graham to Col. John Jordan, 21 February, 1868. *Field Office Records 1865–1872*, ibid.

123. DuBois, 646.

124. Ibid., 135.

125. Leon F. Litwack, *Trouble in Mind: Black Southerners in the Age of Jim Crow* (New York: Alfred A. Knopf: distributed by Random House, 1998), 87.

126. DuBois, 173.

127. Ibid., 166.

Chapter 5

128. Richard Lee Morton, *The Negro in Virginia Politics, 1865–1902* (Charlottesville: University of Virginia Press, 1919), 11.

129. Ibid., 42.

130. Ibid., 44.

131. *The Debates and Proceedings of the Constitutional Convention of the State of Virginia* (Richmond, VA: The New Nation, 1868), 61, https://babel.hathitrust.org/cgi/pt?id=hvd.li14pl;view=1up;seq=67.

132. Ibid.,165,https://babel.hathitrust.org/cgi/pt?id=hvd li14pl;view=1up;seq=171.

133. Ibid., 176, https://babel.hathitrust.org/cgi/pt?id=hvd.li14pl;view=1up;seq=182.

134. Ibid., 195, https://babel.hathitrust.org/cgi/pt?id=hvd.li14pl;view=1up;seq=201.

135. Alrutheus Ambush Taylor, *The Negro in the Reconstruction of Virginia* (Washington, DC: Association for the Study of Negro Life and History, 1926), 58.

136. DuBois, 638.

137. Minority Report of the Committee on the Elective Franchise and Qualifications for Office, Doc. No. 37, *Documents of the Constitutional Convention of the State of Virginia* (Richmond, VA: The New Nation, 1867), 196, https://quod.lib.umich.edu/m/moa/aew7583.0001.001/196.

138. J.N. Brenaman, *A History of Virginia Conventions* (Richmond, VA: J.L. Hill Printing, 1902), 73, https://books.google.com/books?id=Lng1AQAAMAAJ.

139. "Homicide at Charlotte Courthouse—Joe Holmes Killed," *Richmond Dispatch*, May 5, 1869.

140. "The Writ of Habeas Corpus in Virginia," *New York Herald*, June 25, 1869, http://www.infoweb.newsbank.com/iw-search/we/HistArchive.

141. Editorial, *Mecklenburg Herald*, November 2, 1870.

142. "Election Day in Boydton," *Mecklenburg Herald*, November 9, 1870.

143. "The Labor Question," *Mecklenburg Herald*, November 23, 1870.

144. Editorial, *Mecklenburg Herald*, November 30, 1870.

145. "Ninth of April in Boydton," *Mecklenburg Herald*, April 12, 1871.

146. "Why Do Our Farmers Cultivate Tobacco," *Mecklenburg Herald*, May 3, 1871.

147. "A Word of Warning," *Roanoke Valley* (Boydton, VA), January 13, 1872.

148. Foner, 422.

149. "Who Are the Negroes Friends?" *Southside Virginian* (Boydton, VA), July 17, 1873.

150. Cong. H. Comm. on H. Administration Subcomm. on Elections, "List of insolvent capitation and property taxes for the year 1881," Mecklenburg County, Clarksville District, in *Massey vs. Wise: Papers and Testimony in the Contested-Election Case of John E. Massey vs. John S. Wise, from the State of Virginia at Large*, Index to the Miscellaneous Documents of the House of Representatives for the First Session of the Forty-Eighth Congress, 1883–1884, vol. 15, Misc. Doc. No. 27, pt. 2 (Washington: Government Printing Office, 1884), 737, https://books.google.com/books?id=KlFHAQAAIAAJ.

151. Editorial, *Roanoke Valley*, April 27, 1877.

152. Blake, 189.

153. Levin, 60.

154 Blake, 234.

155. Luther Porter Jackson, *Negro Office-Holders in Virginia, 1865–1895* (Norfolk, VA: Guide Quality Press, 1945), 75.

156. Harold S. Forsythe, "But My Friends Are Poor: Ross Hamilton and Freedpeople's Politics in Mecklenburg County, Virginia, 1869–1901," *Virginia Magazine of History and Biography*, vol. 105, no. 4, autumn 1997, 411.

157. "Negro Riot: Bloodshed in the City of Danville," *Richmond Dispatch*, November 4, 1883.

158. *Lynching in America: Confronting the Legacy of Racial Terror,* 3rd ed., (Montgomery, AL: Equal Justice Initiative, 2017), 40.

159. Kiara Boone, Deputy Program Manager, Equal Justice Initiative, e-mail to the author, November 2017.

160. W. Fitzhugh Brundage, *Lynching in the New South: Georgia and Virginia, 1880–1930* (Urbana: University of Illinois Press, 1993), 281.

161. Reprinted in the *Halifax Advertiser* (Halifax Court House, VA), August 9, 1888.

162. Brundage, 281.

163. Ibid., 66.

164. "All Roanoke Is in Mourning: Terrible Result of Last Night's Mob Law," *Roanoke Times*, September 21, 1893.

165. "Peace and Quiet Restored After a Horrible Deed Was Done; Negro Smith's Body Burned," *Roanoke Times*, September 22, 1893.

166. Litwack, *Trouble in Mind*, 308.

167. J. Douglas Smith, *Managing White Supremacy: Race, Politics, and Citizenship in Jim Crow Virginia* (Chapel Hill: University of North Carolina Press, 2002), 176.

168. Billie Holiday, vocal performance of "Strange Fruit," by Lewis Allan, recorded at the Commodore Music Shop in New York City, April 20, 1939, Commodore Records 526-A, 78 rpm.

169. Blake, 246.

170. V.O. Key Jr., *Southern Politics in State and Nation* (New York: Alfred A. Knopf, 1949), 20.

171. Smith, 27.

172. Morton, 159.

173. Ralph Clipman McDanel, *The Virginia Constitutional Convention of 1901–1902* (Baltimore: Johns Hopkins Press, 1928), 154.

Chapter 6

174. Register of Marriages, Mecklenburg County, VA, 1879, p. 233, microfilm, reel 30, Library of Virginia, Richmond.

175. Register of Marriages, Mecklenburg County, VA, 1868, p. 195, microfilm, reel 30, Library of Virginia, Richmond.

176. 1880 US Census, Mecklenburg County, VA, population schedule, Clarksville Township, p. 26, https://www.ancestrylibrary.com.

177. George Sizemore, interview by the author, July 2012.

178. Deed dated 20 November 1903, Mecklenburg County Land Records, Deed Book 69, p. 248, Mecklenburg County Courthouse, Boydton, VA.

179. 1910 US Census, Mecklenburg County, VA, population schedule, Clarksville District, sheet 5B, https://www.ancestrylibrary.com.

180. George D. Wharton in *The Southern Workman*, Hampton Institute, September 1898.

181. George Foster Peabody, "A Negro Pioneer," *New York Tribune*, March 1925.

182. Deed dated 1 December 1919, Mecklenburg County Land Records, Deed Book 85, p. 61, Mecklenburg County Courthouse, Boydton, VA.

183. George D. Wharton, address to the 24th annual session of Bluestone Baptist Sunday School Convention, Drakes Branch, VA, July 1909.

184. Smith, 108.

185. Ibid., 234.

186. 1930 US Census, Passaic County, NJ, population schedule, City of Passaic, Second Ward, sheet 7B, https://www.ancestrylibrary.com.

187. 1920 US Census, Essex County, NJ, population schedule, Town of Nutley, Ward 2, sheet 15A and sheet 27A https://www.ancestrylibrary.com.

188. Howard Sizemore, interview by the author, August 2013.

189. Minnie Arnold, interview by the author, September 2013.

190. John Sizemore, interview by the author, September 2013.

191. Jesse Austin, interview by the author, August 2013.

Chapter 7

192. Rose Shealy, interview by the author, September 2013.

193. John W. Blassingame, *The Slave Community: Plantation Life in the Antebellum South* (New York: Oxford University Press, 1972), 165.

194. DuBois, 44.

195. Jennie Brown to the sheriff of Mecklenburg County, VA, 18 June 1882. Free Negro and Slave Records, 1781–1882. Local Government Records Collection, Mecklenburg County court records, Library of Virginia, Richmond.

Chapter 8

196. Plaque at Robert Russa Moton Museum, Farmville, VA.

197. William Bryan Crawley Jr., *Bill Tuck: A Political Life in Harry Byrd's Virginia* (Charlottesville: University Press of Virginia, 1978), 228.

198. Ibid., 233.

199. Smith, 296.

200. Lynn Briley, remarks given at "Integrating the College of William and Mary," panel discussion at the 6th Annual Lemon Project Symposium, College of William and Mary, March 19, 2016.

201. Daffodil Graham, interview by the author, April 2013.

202. Evella Hutcheson, interview by the author, August 2013.

Chapter 9

203. Howard el-Yasin, interview by the author, September 2013.

204. Dyson, *Dyson Reader*, 235.

205. Michael Eric Dyson, *Tears We Cannot Stop: A Sermon to White America* (New York: St. Martin's Press, 2017), 3.

Chapter 10

206. 1900 US Census, Mecklenburg County, VA, population schedule, Clarksville District, sheet 2A, https://www.ancestrylibrary.com.

207. John d'Entremont, remarks given at "Facing the Past, Freeing the Future: Slavery's Legacy, Freedom's Promise."

208. Rakesh Kochhar and Richard Fry, "Wealth Inequality Has Widened Along Racial, Ethnic Lines Since End of Great Recession," Pew Research Center, December 12, 2014, http://www.pewresearch.org/fact-tank/2014/12/12/racial-wealth-gaps-great-recession.

209. "Poverty Rate by Race/Ethnicity," State Health Facts, Henry J. Kaiser Family Foundation, 2016, accessed November 16, 2017, https://www.kff.org/other/state-indicator/poverty-rate-by-raceethnicity.

210. US Centers for Disease Control and Prevention, *User Guide to the 2015 Period Linked Birth/Infant Death Public Use File*, Table 1, "Infant mortality rates, live births, and infant deaths by selected characteristics and Hispanic origin of mother and by race of mother for mothers of non-Hispanic origin: United States, 2015," p. 79, accessed November 16, 2017, ftp://ftp.cdc.gov/pub/Health_Statistics/NCHS/Dataset_Documentation/DVS/periodlinked/LinkPE15Guide.pdf.

211. Drew DeSilver, "Black Unemployment Rate Is Consistently Twice That of Whites," Pew Research Center, August 21, 2013, http://www.pewresearch.org/fact-tank/2013/08/21/through-good-times-and-bad-black-unemployment-is-consistently-double-that-of-whites.

212. Ryan Gabrielson, Eric Sagara, and Ryann Grochowski Jones, "Deadly Force, in Black and White," ProPublica, October 10, 2014, https://www.propublica.org/article/deadly-force-in-black-and-white.

213. Thomas P. Bonczar, "Prevalence of Imprisonment in the U.S. Population, 1974–2001," US Bureau of Justice Statistics, August 2003, https://www.bjs.gov/content/pub/pdf/piusp01.pdf.

214. NAACP Criminal Justice Fact Sheet, 2015, accessed November 16, 2007, http://www.naacp.org/criminal-justice-fact-sheet.

215. Tom DeWolf, interview by the author, December 2015.

216. Clarence Page, syndicated column, November 9, 2008, reprinted in Clarence Page, *Culture Worrier: Reflections on Race, Politics and Social Change* (Chicago: Bolden, 2014), 37.

217. E-mail received by the author, August 2015.

218. Art Carter, interview by the author, January 2016.

219. Art Carter, remarks given at "Facing the Past, Freeing the Future: Slavery's Legacy, Freedom's Promise."